M000305166

HIDDEN HISTORY
of
MYSTIC &
STONINGTON

HIDDEN HISTORY
of
MYSTIC &
STONINGTON

Gail B. MacDonald

THE
History
PRESS

Published by The History Press
Charleston, SC
www.historypress.com

Copyright © 2020 by Gail B. MacDonald
All rights reserved

Front cover: Courtesy Indian & Colonial Research Center, Incorporated, Old Mystic, Connecticut.
Back cover, top: Courtesy Mystic River Historical Society Inc., Mystic, Connecticut; *bottom*: Courtesy Mystic River Historical Society Inc., Mystic, Connecticut.

First published 2020

Manufactured in the United States

ISBN 9781467140546

Library of Congress Control Number: 2019954379

Notice: The information in this book is true and complete to the best of our knowledge. It is offered without guarantee on the part of the author or The History Press. The author and The History Press disclaim all liability in connection with the use of this book.

All rights reserved. No part of this book may be reproduced or transmitted in any form whatsoever without prior written permission from the publisher except in the case of brief quotations embodied in critical articles and reviews.

To my mom and dad, Doris and Andrew Braccidiferro.
Forever loved. Always missed.

CONTENTS

CONTENTS

ACKNOWLEDGEMENTS

I was first attracted to the Mystic and Stonington area by its rich history attentively tended. I was fortunate to call Pawcatuck—one of Stonington's three major villages—home for twenty-five years. During that time, my appreciation for the community's past grew. I lived in a house built around 1900, located in a neighborhood of century-plus-old houses. West Broad Street School, which opened in 1900, was located a half block away. My daughter attended kindergarten through grade four there.

Also just a short stroll away was the Pawcatuck River, with a history all its own. In 1614, the Dutch explorer Adriaen Block ventured inland on what he called the East River, becoming the first European to do so. A few years later, the colonies of Rhode Island, Connecticut and Massachusetts would almost come to blows over who controlled the waterway and, more important, the land on its banks.

Always interested in exploring how the past shapes the present and prepares us for the future, and having been active in numerous local organizations for years, I began this book project in early 2018 confident of my local history knowledge. I quickly realized, however, that what I knew only scratched the surface. I had much to learn and now, as the project is completed, have many to thank for their invaluable assistance in this process.

My deepest gratitude goes first to all those whose mission it is to keep history alive: those at the Stonington Historical Society, Mystic River Historical Society, Westerly Historical Society, local history archives at the Groton Public Library and the Indian and Colonial Research Center.

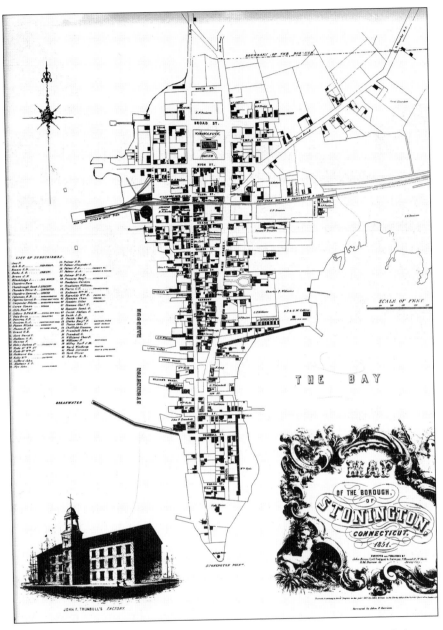

Map of Stonington Borough from 1845. *Courtesy collection of the Stonington Historical Society.*

West Main Street, Mystic, looking west, late 1800s. Union Baptist Church is at the top of the hill. *Courtesy Mystic River Historical Society Inc., Mystic, Connecticut.*

All were helpful beyond belief. A special thanks to Chelsea Ordner at the Stonington Historical Society's Richard W. Woolworth Library and Research Center and Dorrie Hanna at the Mystic River Historical Society for their repeated assistance in my research. More thanks go to those who oversee the archives at the Mystic Seaport Museum, the research center at the Connecticut Historical Society and the special collections at Connecticut College. The resources in all of these archives were vital to uncovering some of the richest stories of the region's past.

Many individuals also deserve my sincere thanks. One of the most difficult parts of this project was deciding what stories to tell and recognizing that, in choosing what to include in this volume, much would also be left out. There was an almost unlimited number of interesting stories from which to choose, after all. Countless unique characters and significant people have called Mystic and Stonington home. For helping me narrow my focus and elucidate stories about which I was previously unaware, I am deeply indebted to David Erskine, Blanche Higgins, Marilyn Comrie, Mary Beth Baker, Carol Sommer, Cedric Woods and Larry O'Keefe.

Every writer also needs editors. Many thanks to David Erskine, Mary Beth Baker, Marilyn Comrie and my husband, Bruce MacDonald, for reading early drafts of the manuscript. They all helped correct mistakes, smooth out writing and direct the storytelling in a more engaging and historically appropriate manner. These editors helped me with context, informed me of holes in the narrative and suggested changes. All these editors share not only a great eye for detail, but also a deep love for Stonington and Mystic and a wealth of knowledge about local history.

I also need to offer extra thanks to my husband for compiling the index for this book. My deepest love and gratitude to Bruce—I couldn't have done it without you.

INTRODUCTION

Mystic and its environs are among New England's top tourist destinations. But many visitors to the two top local attractions have no idea they are in the town of Stonington when they visit Mystic Seaport or Mystic Aquarium.

Mystic is actually a village spanning two towns. The section of the village east of the Mystic River is part of the town of Stonington, while the part of the village west of the river lies in the town of Groton. Mystic includes the areas around the seaport and aquarium, along with the thriving downtown with its iconic drawbridge.

Mystic is just one, albeit the best known, of Stonington's three major villages. The Borough of Stonington, also called the Village, is home to the town's commercial fishing fleet, the 1823 lighthouse museum and many beautiful historic homes. Pawcatuck lies at the eastern edge of town and has long been tied economically and culturally to its Rhode Island neighbor, the town of Westerly.

Not only do Mystic and Stonington encompass more geography than what is widely understood, but the communities also possess a depth and breadth that goes well beyond the stock images on tourist brochures. These are lively and diverse communities with long histories and an ever-changing landscape. Long the domain of native tribes, the region's first European settlers established a trading post on the Pawcatuck River in 1649. Just thirteen years after the trading post was established, four European settlers—Thomas Stanton, William Chesebrough, Walter Palmer and Thomas Miner—founded the town.

From humble beginnings, the region grew to an economic powerhouse of shipyards and sea-dependent businesses. It also was a transportation hub, an industrial center and a seat of commerce and finance. A long list of explorers, sea captains, inventors, industrialists, shipbuilders, financiers and other power brokers called Mystic and Stonington home. Artists and poets were also drawn to the region.

Many notable locals achieved much, and their accomplishments brought great distinction to the communities. The clipper ships built in Mystic shipyards revolutionized international trade and, beginning in 1849, set speed records bringing to California those seeking fortunes in the gold rush. The merchant ships, whalers and sealing vessels made many people wealthy. A local notable, Nathaniel Palmer, is credited with first sighting Antarctica. Much later, Italian tenor Sergio Franchi and Pulitzer Prize–winning poet James Merrill both called Stonington home.

Many of these noteworthy citizens and their accomplishments have been thoroughly documented by others. This book instead turns to other people, places and events influential in shaping the unique character of contemporary Mystic and Stonington. For example, the book focuses on the

West Broad Street, Pawcatuck, early 1900s. Several of the buildings pictured remain today. *Courtesy Westerly Library & Wilcox Park.*

immigrant manufacturing workers instead of the factory owners and on the ships' crews instead of the ships' owners.

Much of the success of Stonington's railroad and steamboats was possible because of African American workers. Much local history and a large swath of Mystic land are preserved thanks to women. Many locally pivotal events are now nearly lost in the fog of history.

Much of this more hidden history of Stonington and Mystic I discovered thanks to the dedicated local history keepers at historical societies and archives. Some I pieced together through the eyes of local journalists, who are, as *Washington Post* publisher Donald Graham once said, chroniclers of the "first rough draft of history." This journey of discovery was enlightening for me. More important, however, is sharing these tales about the people and events vital not only to Stonington's and Mystic's past, but also to its present and future as well.

NATIVES' LAND

The area now called Mystic and Stonington was controlled by the Pequot Indians until the early seventeenth century. They frequently camped along the shoreline, where they caught fish, clams and other shellfish. But when more and more Europeans began making their homes in the region, tensions between natives and settlers increased.

On the night of May 26, 1637, a militia of some ninety well-armed colonial troops under the direction of John Mason sought to end the Pequots' attacks on white settlements. The militia launched a surprise strike on the tribal fort strategically located at the top of a hill on the west side of the Mystic River, near where Pequot Avenue today reaches its crest. Many of the natives were asleep. Most were unable to escape. The colonials set the fort ablaze. Between four hundred and seven hundred Pequots, including women, the elderly and young children, were killed. The few who managed to escape were taken prisoner and enslaved.

After the massacre at the Mystic fort, an event considered pivotal in the Pequot War, white settlers considered the tribe officially extinct. Surviving tribal members were reduced to living in slavery or abject poverty. Desperate Native American parents sometimes agreed to allow their children to be indentured. In these agreements, the parent got a small payment in return for allowing the child to be an enslaved worker for a particular person for an agreed-on number of years.

In 1651, the remaining Pequots were granted a five-hundred-acre reservation in what is now the village of Noank, just west of Mystic. But in

Captain John Mason's troops massacred Pequot men, women and children in Mystic in 1637. This Mason statue stood for more than a century near the site of the Pequot fort. *Courtesy of the Indian & Colonial Research Center Inc., Old Mystic, Connecticut.*

a pattern that would be played out again and again through the course of American history, in 1666, the tribe was dispossessed of the Noank property. The Western Pequot, also called the Mashantucket Pequot, reservation located about twelve miles from the coast, then was granted to the tribe.

Those tribal members who chose to stay in the town of Groton lived in such deplorable conditions that by 1766 a group of European settlers had petitioned the colonial government in Hartford to be allowed to study the Groton Indians. The settlers later reported that about 150 natives lived locally and recommended the Indians might find relief from their plight if they agreed to become Christians.

By the mid-1800s, many native men in southeastern Connecticut sought to improve their conditions by heading to sea as crew members aboard whaling ships. While the job was dirty and dangerous and officials sometimes resorted to coercion to secure their crews, American Indians and African Americans found commercial ships to be places where they could be valued for the quality of their work and treated equally to their fellow sailors.

It wouldn't be until the late 1900s that members of New England's native tribes began to regain some of their previous wealth, power and respect. Both the Mashantucket Pequot and Mohegan tribes opened southeastern Connecticut casinos on their ancestral lands just miles from Stonington and Mystic, sparking a remarkable transformation of the area and turning the once poverty-stricken tribes into economic powerhouses. Figures provided by the state of Connecticut show that in direct payments alone, the tribes contributed $7.5 billion to Hartford through 2017.

WHALERS

Elisha Apes endured plenty of hardships during three grueling whaling voyages by the late 1830s. On his fourth voyage, however, he decided the injustices aboard the New London, Connecticut–based *Ann Maria* were more than he could bear. The captain mercilessly bullied a young cabin boy, who, like Apes, was Native American. Apes was especially pained when the boy was forced to stand on the ship's foretop in the freezing cold for an extended period.

Apes and the ship's carpenter, William Gilbert, angrily confronted the captain about the cruel behavior. That confrontation put the whalemen in a no-win position aboard the ship. So, when the *Ann Maria* sailed within sight of the coast of New Zealand, Apes and Gilbert left the ship. They lived out their lives in New Zealand with numerous others who joined local people there.

Nancy Shoemaker tells Apes's story in her book *Living with Whales: Documents and Oral Histories of Native New England Whaling History*. Apes was a Pequot Indian who spent his boyhood just outside the village of Mystic and, as did many Native Americans of his time, went to sea aboard whaling ships. He left on his first voyage when he was just seventeen.

Apes was born around 1815, 178 years after the Pequots were massacred by John Mason's troops in Mystic. During the eighteenth and nineteenth centuries, there is much evidence that members of the once powerful tribes were held as slaves in Stonington. In 1750, there were 930 Indians listed as slaves throughout the state of Connecticut, and at the time of the American Revolution, New London County had about a third of all the slaves who lived in the state.

In 1766, the Stonington selectmen avoided paying for the support of an Indian woman by binding her out to a resident named William Gallup. The 1810 census for Stonington lists Thomas Cinnamon, a "mulatto" born in 1795, and Robbin, "an Indian man," among the residents. The term *mulatto* was often used in early records to describe those with Native American or mixed ancestry.

Native Americans faced intense bigotry throughout the seventeenth, eighteenth and nineteenth centuries. Only the most menial and demeaning jobs were available to them. Serving on whaling and sealing ships offered minorities an opportunity to earn better wages than they could in port. There also was more racial acceptance aboard ships.

While he was not a Stonington resident, Paul Cuffe was a Pequot Indian whose story illustrates both the opportunities and hardships natives might find at sea during this era. Born in Westport, Massachusetts, in the last years of the eighteenth century, he headed to sea at age twelve in 1808 aboard a cargo ship shuttling apples, cotton, rice and lumber among northern U.S. ports; Savannah, Georgia; and northern Europe.

Cuffe sailed the world and rose to prominence as one of the wealthiest men of color in the country. He became a ship's captain, businessman and prominent abolitionist. In an 1839 booklet titled *Narrative of the Life and Adventure of Paul Cuffe, A Pequot Indian*, he also describes some of the hardships. During the War of 1812, for example, he was among nine hundred American sailors held by the British in dismal conditions on a prison ship. He survived for about a year aboard the ship, enduring meager rations, scourges of yellow fever and even recapture after he jumped overboard in an effort to escape. Around 1835, he witnessed three fellow whalemen killed when their boat was struck by a whale. Cuffe finally made it back to New England in 1836.

Many Pequots and members of other native tribes in southeastern Connecticut worked as whalemen on ships sailing from Mystic and Stonington. Others headed to the larger whaling ports of New Bedford, Massachusetts, and New London, Connecticut.

Mystic became a whaling port in 1832, when George Bingham sailed out of the village and returned nine months later with 550 barrels of whale oil valued at $4,500. Over the next thirty years, twenty-eight vessels made 103 whaling voyages out of Mystic. Stonington's foray into whaling began with the 1821 voyage of the sloop *Essex*, which returned to port from the Shetland Islands with 200 barrels of whale oil, along with a quantity of seal skins. Between 1821 and 1892, fifty-one Stonington vessels took 177 whaling voyages. Both whaling and sealing were vital to the regional economy throughout the nineteenth century.

Many whalemen were illiterate and had little or no experience at sea. Being a member of a whaling crew was not a highly coveted position; sometimes, captains resorted to coercion to secure enough men for their voyages. The crew of about thirty men was expected to follow orders without question and was forced to live together in a space of about 2,500 square feet for extended periods of time. Many contemporary single-family homes in Stonington and Mystic are about this size.

Captains could order a crew member he deemed guilty of disobedience not only to forfeit salary but also to pay for a replacement crew member should one be needed. Walter Coelho, in a 1971 thesis about the Stonington whaling fleet, wrote, "Perhaps no other maritime pursuit asked so much of a man, enduring unbelievable hardships, sailing for months on end without sight of land, and gambling lives in physical combat with the mightiest monsters since the age of dinosaurs."

Native Americans from many tribes, including both Pequots and Mohegans, were employed aboard whaling and sealing ships from the industry's beginning. One typical crew list from 1848 has three "colored" Americans, five natives, two Irish and six Portuguese among the crew. Most crew members endured an average of just three years working on the whalers; a certain number of crew members jumped ship when the vessels pulled into ports to re-provision.

This was the choice Elisha Apes made. He left the *Ann Maria*, although, at the time he abandoned it, the ship was about as far away from New England as is possible to be on the globe. Apes, whose older brother William was a Methodist minister known as a notable orator in New England, married a native Maori woman in New Zealand. The couple had eight children.

Apes introduced land-based whaling in New Zealand, and his descendants became well-known both as whalers and sheepherders. A 1938 obituary for Elisha's son James Apes in a Dunedin, New Zealand newspaper notes: "Shore whaling, as distinct from bay whaling, flourished along the southeastern coastline during the third, fourth and fifth decades of last century. It was to this period that Apes, the original, if he may be so called, belonged. His son,

James Apes, followed his father's footsteps in an industry that took on a new lease of life in the 70s and 80s. He was one of a hardy band that is no longer to be found around our shores."

A shorter obituary for James Apes in another newspaper reported, "Being a man of excellent judgment he was frequently called on to represent the Maori people at important gatherings or to act for them in business matters."

While a life aboard a Connecticut whaleship afforded Elisha Apes a work environment in which he was accepted as an equal, his choice to challenge the ship's captain and then to leave the vessel led him and his children to a life of more prominence and status in New Zealand than would have been likely for him in the United States.

Meeting Lincoln

By the early 1900s, conventional wisdom in Connecticut held that the Native Americans—more commonly known at that time as Indians—were long gone from the region. Although by the early decades of the twentieth century, members of the Mohegan and Pequot tribes continued to live in modest abodes on local reservations and the Narragansetts maintained a relatively strong presence in nearby Rhode Island, teachers throughout the area commonly taught that the great woodland tribes of Connecticut were wiped out during colonial times.

That is likely why, when a *Hartford Courant* reporter in 1927 interviewed at length a Stonington native named Isaac Stanton Mullen, the reporter clearly was in awe. Not only was this descendent of the Mohegans alive and well, but the man also was well spoken, highly educated and widely read. Mullen served in the navy in the years before and during the Civil War and shook President Lincoln's hand after a musical performance in which Mullen participated. Mullen later was the adjutant of the Boston post of the GAR, a veterans' organization for those who served in the Grand Army of the Republic.

The headline labeled Mullen, who said he was eighty-seven at the time of the interview, the "Last of the Mohicans," in a reference to the James Fenimore Cooper novel. The lengthy article describes in great detail an extraordinary life by any measure but one made more so because societal norms of the era stereotyped people of color.

Mullen, a longtime resident of Boston, was born in Stonington in 1840 and spent his early childhood in the village. His mother was a Mohegan whose first marriage was to a member of the Stanton family. That husband was a descendant of one of the first European settlers of the town. Mullen's father, his mother's second husband, was a descendant of a Revolutionary War soldier.

"I can remember those childhood days at Stonington as though they were of the present decade," he is quoted in the article as saying, referring to the 1840s.

> *There was a steamboat line from Stonington to New York in those days and I used to play down on the wharf. I believe this line was one of the most important in this section of the country at the time and Stonington was quite a well-known port. It was my greatest delight to get to the wharf when one of the steamers arrived. My mother used to be discouraged with me and more than one royal battle we had when my five-year-old spirit rebelled at being held home when those steamer whistles sounded.*
>
> *These steamer officials and crews used to think I was quite a novelty. I was just an Indian kid with coarse, straight and black hair down to my waist. They used to plague me about these feet of mine. Of course, they were nothing of this size then, but they were very, very large flat feet for a small child. They brought me candy, they told me stories and I loved those rough men very much.*

Mullen's mother took him from Stonington when he was just six years old. She wanted him to have the best education possible, he said, and so brought him to Boston. Boston had a thriving African American community and was at the forefront of the abolitionist movement at the time. While Mullen was not African American, Native Americans were considered people of color and often found more acceptance in African American communities.

Despite Boston's relatively progressive racial attitudes, its school system was strictly segregated. The school for African American children had few resources, so Mullen's mother moved on to Salem, Massachusetts. She enrolled her son in school there.

Mullen dedicated much of the *Hartford Courant* interview to relaying stories about what he said was his proudest accomplishment: his navy service. He enlisted at age nineteen, around 1859, and served aboard the frigate *Portsmouth*. His service first brought him to the west coast of Africa, where the ship was engaged in intercepting illegal slave ships.

"We were hunting slave smugglers, attempting to break down the traffic," Mullen told the *Courant*. "As a rule, all the slaves taken were from eight to eighteen years of age. It was a terrible traffic and often the slaves were thrown overboard to the sharks for the amusement of the crew of the slave runners, also to stop the spread of disease aboard the ship."

One of Mullen's most vivid memories from his days in the navy occurred at the height of the Civil War. In 1863, he said, Abraham Lincoln and other notables paid a visit to the Union fleet off Hampton Roads, Virginia. A makeshift orchestra consisting of a banjo player, an accordion player and Mullen playing the so-called bones—an instrument that could be a pair of actual animal rib bones or thin cylinders carved from wood—played some lively folk tunes, much to the distinguished audience's delight.

"Seated on the top of three overturned nail kegs, we presently found ourselves the center of a densely packed circle over which towered the tall form of the president," Mullen said, adding that he had become a notable bones player as part of a popular minstrel group that toured in New England in the mid-nineteenth century. "The president was clapping in time with the rhythm, and dignified generals, cabinet members and congressmen joined in the singing, shuffling their feet, clapping, rocking to the music and cheering us three."

Best of all for Mullen was that, after the performance, Lincoln made a point to shake the musician's hand and briefly speak to him. "It wasn't much, but it was great to me," Mullen said. "You see, I was just an Indian and I looked upon Lincoln as the great white father."

Mullen told the reporter that, following the war, he married and had three children. However, by the time of the interview, he said that all of his children and his wife had died.

Other accounts of Mullen and his life are not readily available, which is hardly a surprise given how little attention minorities were afforded by the mainstream press for much of U.S. history. It's also unclear exactly when Mullen died. Still, many of the details of what he relayed to the *Courant* can be corroborated as historically accurate. It's also clear that Connecticut meant a great deal to Mullen. Although he was well into his eighties when the article was published, he indicated that he still planned a trip to his boyhood home.

"It will probably be my last visit to the scenes of my childhood and while I would give a great deal to be able to spend the last days of this life midst the scenes of my childhood, conditions say I must remain here in Boston," he said. "But Boston is a great city, I have spent fifty years of my life here and I ought to know. But, even so, it's as dear to me as old Connecticut."

2

PERSEVERANCE AMID PREJUDICE

On December 6, 1820, a Stonington mother brought her nine-year-old son to a local storekeeper and struck a deal. The store's general account book notes that the store's owner, Thomas Noyes, took George Perry, "a black boy," as an indentured servant that day. Perry would work for Noyes until he was eighteen years old.

What is not revealed in the account book notation, which reads as just another business transaction, is the poverty and lack of options that no doubt led the mother to take this desperate step. Her likely feelings of anguish and the boy's fear also are not revealed. But, of course, this is understood.

Many African Americans lived in the Mystic and Stonington area, mostly as enslaved people, from the time of the earliest European settlers. Like many of the poor whites they lived among, both slaves and free blacks experienced difficult lives. Their days were filled with unrelenting physical labor, and they lived in near obscurity.

Against these odds, some local African Americans achieved remarkable accomplishments. For example, Venture Smith, whose life has been widely chronicled, was born in West Africa and sold into slavery. He was enslaved for a time in Stonington, where he worked for Thomas Stanton II on what is now known as the Davis Farm in lower Pawcatuck. Smith eventually bought his freedom and land near the Connecticut River. Of the nearly twelve million Africans who were brought to the Americas, he was one of only about a dozen former slaves who left behind a firsthand account of the betrayal and cruelty he experienced as a slave. His life story was published in New London, Connecticut, in 1798.

Many African Americans and Native Americans, groups that were pushed to the margins of white-dominated society, went to sea as members of whaling or sealing crews. Peter Harvey, a black man from Stonington, sailed with Nathaniel Palmer in 1820 on a sealing voyage during which Palmer became the first American to sight Antarctica.

A small black community thrived in Stonington Borough during the mid- and late nineteenth century. Blacks worked on the railroad and steamships that transformed Stonington into a transportation hub for travelers going between New York and Boston beginning in 1837. While black children earlier attended school with their white neighbors in Stonington, by the 1860s, a separate "colored" school operated on Broad Street in the borough. An 1867 school register shows twenty-five students between the ages of four and seventeen enrolled there.

In the period before the Civil War, a relatively strong abolitionist sentiment existed in the community, fueled largely by the beliefs of Rogerene Quakers and Seventh Day Baptists. At least two Underground Railroad stops are said to have existed in town—one was the home of prominent Mystic shipyard owner George Greenman, and the other was a house on Liberty Street in Pawcatuck. Because the railroad had to operate in secret, it's difficult to definitively document precise locations of safe homes. But even abolitionists did not necessarily believe in racial equality. Many were proponents of sending blacks back to Africa, although most African Americans had never seen Africa by this point in history and considered themselves Americans. Other whites wanted free blacks to be strictly segregated from whites.

Despite persistent racial prejudice, many blacks became integral members of the local community. Just two examples from a much later era are the Reverend Simon Peter Montgomery and railroad porter Chester W. Walker. In 1955, Montgomery became the country's first black pastor of an all-white congregation when he was appointed to the Old Mystic Methodist Church. Walker died while trying to rescue train passengers during the 1938 hurricane.

THE GABRIELS

Claude and Prudence Jenkins Gabriel climbed as high on the early nineteenth-century socioeconomic ladder as was possible for African Americans. Still, the top rung of that ladder was not very high. They remained servants their entire lives, albeit for some very famous and influential people. In Stonington, their connection to those people afforded them a status as minor celebrities.

Prudence Jenkins Gabriel was the daughter of slaves in Stonington. Her mother was Phillis Brown, who was owned by Captain Peleg Brown. Her father was Pero Hallam, a slave owned by John Hallam. Both her parents' surnames, as was common with slaves, were that of their owners. Pero's other Stonington owner was Thomas Noyes. It's not certain whether this was the same Noyes who held George Perry as an indentured child servant.

Prudence was a free person of color working as a chambermaid in Providence, Rhode Island, when she met Claude Gabriel. Gabriel, a Haitian who came to the United States in about 1800, was a free man and worked in kitchens in Providence.

The couple married, and their reputation as reliable and skilled servants brought them into the employ of numerous notable families in New England. Claude Gabriel, for example, worked for William Jones, the eighth governor of Rhode Island (1811–17). Claude was a waiter and coachman in the governor's household. Prudence worked for the governor's daughter, Harriet Dunn Jones Hoppin.

In the early 1800s, Claude Gabriel sailed to Russia with his employers, and in 1810, he was reported as missing. In reality, the Russian emperor, Alexander, was so impressed with Claude's skills that he asked Claude to stay in Russia and work for him. Claude accepted the work but asked permission to return to the United States to fetch his wife and children and bring them back to Russia with him. Future U.S. president John Quincy Adams, who was serving as U.S. ambassador to Russia at the time, secured Claude's return to Providence in April 1812, along with the subsequent passage back to Russia for Claude, Prudence and their two children.

In early April 1812, Claude and Prudence visited Stonington so that Prudence could see her parents before the journey. Stonington residents long remembered the excitement of this visit. The locals recalled the pageantry of seeing a couple bound to live with royalty. For Prudence, however, the visit was heartbreaking. Overseas travel in the early nineteenth century often meant saying goodbye forever to loved ones. She recorded her feelings in an April 6, 1812 letter to her mother in Stonington. "I cannot leave without again writing to you to express my great sorrow that it has so happened I cannot be favored with seeing you again," she wrote. "It is reasonable to suppose that I shall never more behold my dear parents' faces in this life."

She tells her mother that a free mulatto woman will travel with them. The woman will be a comfort to the family, most notably because of her ability to read and write. Prudence begs her mother to write to her, noting that her mother can send letters via the ships that sail to Russia each spring from Providence, New York and Boston.

"I herewith send you a dark colored muff and tipet," Prudence writes. "Which I want you to accept in remembrance of me which I send as a token of my affection."

While the Gabriels' Stonington visit made a splash, the written record of the family appears to dead end there. Prudence clearly understood that she would not return to Stonington. "I hope we may be permitted to meet again in a future state," Prudence writes, referring to a time after their respective deaths.

A CHURCH OF THEIR OWN

On November 10, 1849, a Stonington publication called the *Extinguisher* reported, "We are rejoiced that our colored population have now a place where they can worship without fear or molestation." A month earlier, a small group of African American residents secured permission from Stonington's First Baptist Church to form its own congregation. The Third Baptist Church, always cash poor and often with just a tiny number of congregants, survived for some seventy years in a neat, white clapboard building on Water Street in Stonington Borough.

A group of eight residents, most of whom were members of the Ross family, petitioned to form the new church. The family was well known in Stonington; one member, Allen Ross, became an accomplished artist locally by the 1880s. While the newspaper article mentioned the congregants could then worship without fear or molestation, there actually is little evidence of how Stonington's African Americans lived or how they were treated by the more powerful and larger white community. It's also unclear whether they petitioned to form their own church because they felt unwelcome or uneasy in the First Baptist congregation, or simply because they felt most comfortable and freer when they were with other African Americans. What is more certain, however, is that, given both the laws and prevailing societal attitudes of the day, it's highly likely that members of Stonington's black community encountered healthy doses of both disdain and racism, at least at some points in their lives.

In general, the mid-nineteenth century was a time when black residents were persecuted and subjugated, even in states such as Connecticut, where slavery was prohibited. In addition, Connecticut was far from a hotbed of progressive thinking when it came to racial matters. It lagged behind many of its New England neighbors by outlawing slavery only in 1848, just a year before Stonington's Third Baptist Church was formed.

Slavery was fairly common in Connecticut and throughout the American colonies from the earliest days of European settlement. By 1774, there were 6,562 slaves in Connecticut, according to information in *The Underground Railroad in Connecticut* by Horatio T. Strother. By 1790, the number of slaves in the state had declined to 2,759. Another 2,801 residents were listed as free blacks.

In Stonington, many of the early European settlers and wealthiest families in town were slaveholders. The 1747 estate of Daniel Denison of Stonington, for example, shows that along with cows, oxen, swine and horses, Denison listed among his possessions "one negro man named Jack," "one negro woman named Ruth" and two "negro girls" named Philis and Sibbina. Thomas Wheeler's 1755 inventory lists fifteen slaves among his possessions. In 1761, Prudence Potter Williams's will left to heirs "my negro man named Derrick, my negro woman named Jenny," along with "my riding mare, my two cows and a calf."

By 1800, a time when it was still common to see advertisements in local newspapers seeking the return of runaway slaves, three local families—the Williamses, Gallups and Wheelers—had begun to emancipate their slaves. By that time, slaves could not be sold in the state, and older slaves became economic burdens. Gradual emancipation laws beginning in 1784 listed children born to enslaved parents as free, although they remained under their parents' and parents' owners' control until they were adults.

At least a few local black residents gained wide respect in the community. Quash Williams is one, for example. Williams was a local slave emancipated in 1795 who became well known in the area as a lay preacher at the Second Baptist Church on Fort Hill in Groton, just a few miles west of Mystic. Decades after his death in 1830, the public paid for a marble slab to mark his grave in Mystic's Whitehall Cemetery. An epitaph on the marker reads, "Old Quash was truly an example."

As the nineteenth century progressed, the abolitionist movement grew in parts of Connecticut, especially among certain religious groups. The Quakers took a very early stand against slavery, although some of their members much earlier were active in the slave trade. Prominent Seventh

Day Baptists such as the Greenmans in Mystic, along with members of the Pawcatuck Seventh Day Baptist church, located just east of the Connecticut–Rhode Island border in Westerly, Rhode Island, were active in the abolition movement. Some church members, including the Greenmans, likely hosted stops on the Underground Railroad, providing shelter to those who escaped enslavement in southern states and headed to freedom in Canada.

Outside of abolitionist circles, attitudes about blacks were generally harsh. Many in Connecticut, for example, stood firmly against abolition, and abolitionist speakers were frequently taunted, booed and pummeled with rotten produce, as happened to one speaker who came to Mystic.

In Canterbury, about thirty miles inland from Stonington, Prudence Crandall was terrorized by her neighbors after she set up a school for black girls in the early 1830s. The state legislature passed a so-called Black Law in 1833 prohibiting the education of out-of-state black children without advance permission from residents of the town where the school was to be located. Connecticut legislator Andrew Judson wrote about the Black Law: "We are not merely opposed to the establishment of that school in Canterbury; we mean there shall be no such a school set up anywhere in our state. The colored people can never rise from their menial condition in our country; they ought not to be permitted to rise here. They are an inferior race of beings, and never can or ought to be recognized as the equal of whites." Ironically, in 1840, Judson was the federal district judge who ruled in favor of the *Amistad* mutineers, saying in that ruling they should be freed and returned to Africa.

It was amid such sentiments, and at a time when their ranks were on the increase, that the free blacks in Stonington petitioned to form their own church. The village's transformation into a bustling hub of commerce and transportation in the mid-nineteenth century brought many African Americans to the borough. They came to work in a variety of capacities for the railroad and steamship lines, as well as in farming, on the docks, at the Wadawanuck Hotel and as servants in private homes. The 1850 census lists seventy-four black or mulatto residents over the age of sixteen living in the borough. Many more spent time in the village between their ships' voyages or trains' journeys.

The Third Baptist reported each June to the larger church organization, the Stonington Union Association, or SUA. These reports chronicle the church's evolution and its challenges. In 1851, Third Baptist formed a church school; thirty children attended religious education classes there. It took three years for the members of Third Baptist to pay off the meetinghouse debt. But, in 1855, the church reported that it had lost its pastor. It would have no regular pastor for the next four years. Throughout the church's history, it struggled to retain a permanent pastor.

With the Civil War raging in 1862, Third Baptist reported that its membership stood at fifty. It also reported to the SUA, "We are not indifferent spectators of the dreadful strife now raging in our country." Two members of the congregation had themselves been slaves.

Two years after the war's end, in perhaps the ultimate chiding of local societal sentiment, the church reported: "We are glad liberty has been proclaimed thru-out the land, and we are anxiously looking for the day when colored people of Connecticut shall enjoy equal privileges with the Freedmen of the South; when Connecticut shall be as free as South Carolina."

As long as Stonington remained a railroad and steamship hub, a community of African Americans remained in the village and the Third Baptist Church survived, even in years when it struggled with a dwindling congregation, endured sickness among congregants or suffered financial woes.

By the turn of the twentieth century, however, the African American community decreased sharply. By 1917, the church reported to the SUA that it was considering ceasing operation, noting it had just three members left. By 1924, the church could no longer hold on. A committee to disband was formed, and church property was sold at auction in 1926.

After the sale, the church building was moved. It was rolled down Water Street and across the railroad tracks to a lot where it served as home to the newly formed Stonington Fire District and later to the Knights of Columbus, a Catholic fraternal organization. In January 1966, the building was destroyed by fire.

Even with the church gone, members of the families who worshipped there remained. Stiles H.F. Ross, for example, a member of the family that founded Third Baptist Church and a congregant until the church was disbanded and sold, lived in the village until he died at age ninety-six in 1954. His obituary in *The Day* of New London notes that he was the town's oldest resident at the time of his death and was dedicated to public service in the village. He began working as a cabin boy aboard the *Skipper* while still a child. He and his wife ran a catering business and a popular ice cream stand in the village for many years. Ross also served as tax collector and assessor for the Stonington Fire District. When he retired from that

The railroad and steamships transformed Stonington into a busy, noisy industrial center in the nineteenth century. *G.A. Hyde postcard, courtesy Mystic Seaport Museum.*

Today's Town Dock in Stonington Borough was the steamboat dock beginning in the mid-1800s. *Postcard image courtesy Mystic Seaport Museum.*

Steamboat Landing, Stonington, Conn.

Above: The steamboat dock and railroad yards made Stonington Borough a busy, noisy industrial village in the second half of the nineteenth century. *Courtesy Stonington Historical Society, Dorothea Hewitt Gould Collection.*

Left: The Third Baptist Church was built by Stonington's African American community. It was located in the borough from 1849 until 1926. *Courtesy Stonington Historical Society, Dorothea Hewitt Gould Collection.*

role in 1952, he was the oldest tax collector in the country, and his work was praised by state auditors.

His obituary also recalled that most local residents recognized him, as for many years he took a daily walk through the village. With his beloved Third Baptist Church long gone by the time of his death, Ross's funeral service was instead held at the Second Congregational Church.

Serving the Traveling Public

For more than thirty years in the middle of the twentieth century, the sumptuous summer Sunday dinners at Orchard House, an inn in the Pawcatuck section of Stonington, drew diners from many miles to the farthest corner of southeastern Connecticut. With a backdrop of soft dinner music playing, women dressed in their Sunday finery and men in suits and ties gathered to eat lobster and chicken with stuffed tomatoes, coleslaw, baked macaroni and vegetables, all topped off with homemade desserts.

About thirty diners were guests of the inn. Another thirty day-trippers from New Haven, Hartford and other locales joined them. All the guests, along with the inn's owners and employees, were African American.

Life for African Americans was improving as the twentieth century progressed. Still, they continued to face many unpleasant everyday realities. While lynchings, Jim Crow laws and the prevalence of the Ku Klux Klan made their lives much more dangerous in southern states, even in the North, institutionalized practices, the prevalence of racial prejudices and some long-standing laws made it difficult for them to travel freely, buy homes where they wanted, secure high-paying jobs, get equal education for their children and exercise their right to vote.

The growing African American middle and professional classes, for example, wanted to join in on the increasingly popular trend of automobile travel. Even when they could afford to own a car, however, many feared the consequences of wandering to parts unknown. In 1936, the *Negro Motorist Green Book* began annual publication to allow African Americans more freedom to travel. It listed hotels, restaurants, gas stations and other businesses where they would be welcomed.

Other businesses became well known through word of mouth. In Stonington, the Orchard House was one such place.

Minnie Carter and her sister Gertrude Owens opened the Orchard House, first on Liberty Street in the village of Pawcatuck in 1938 in a building that previously was home to the Durgin Spaghetti House, Carter told reporter Marilyn Comrie for an article in the *Westerly Sun* in February 1994. Carter, who said she worked as a clerk for the Urban League and as a waitress in Brooklyn, New York, before establishing the business in southeastern Connecticut, often heard complaints from African American professionals that too many of the hotels and restaurants that welcomed them offered subpar conditions, food and service.

Carter and Owens set out to change this. The Liberty Street inn offered five guest rooms and was open from late July through Labor Day. After operating there for several years, the sisters began looking for a larger place. In 1946, they settled on a traditional New England–style inn on Route 1 that had first operated as the White House Inn.

That inn had fifteen guest rooms and a dining room in a separate building. It was located west of the village of Pawcatuck, in an area that at the time was considered somewhat remote. Indeed, the isolation of the location was a main reason that residents argued against building a new Stonington High School there in the 1930s. About twenty years later, a new high school was built, however, directly across Route 1 from the site of the Orchard House Inn. Stonington High remains in that location today, although the Orchard House is long gone.

At the age of ninety, Minnie Carter recalled, in telling the story of the Orchard House, that a Mrs. Van Allen, owner of the White House Inn, was delighted to sell her business to Carter and Owens. "Her lawyer advised against it," Carter said. "But she wanted us to have the place."

The neighbors were not so delighted.

After the sale was finalized, Carter said she became aware that a group of neighbors had circulated a petition to keep Carter and her sister from operating the inn. The petition was based solely on racial prejudice. While the sisters initially got a chilly reception from their neighbors, guests fell in love with the place and the quality of food, lodging and service it provided. By the mid-1940s, most guests made annual visits. The guests were primarily professionals—lawyers, physicians, teachers and other white-collar, middle-class African Americans.

Besides enjoying elegant Sunday dinners, the inn guests played bridge, shuffleboard, croquet and Ping-Pong and motored around the shoreline area, enjoying the scenery and beaches.

By the early 1970s, the character of the neighborhood had changed. Route 1 was busier, noisier and certainly less remote. Commercial development spread to the area. Racial barriers were coming down, so accommodations catering to blacks were less in demand. The Orchard House was sold and later demolished.

Older residents still recall the polite and genteel guests who stayed at the Orchard House and the proprietors who worked hard to ensure it was a quality lodging and dining facility. The stone pillars that once marked the entrance to the inn still stand not far from the town's police headquarters, the only reminder of a time when, even locally, racial segregation was the practice, if not the law.

3
Forgotten Places in a Changing Landscape

Even in a community known for astute preservation of its past, the landscape changes dramatically over more than three hundred years of history. Today's genteel Stonington village was once a noisy, smelly and crowded railroad and steamboat terminus. Armies of workers once trudged down streets in Pawcatuck, Mystic and Stonington on their way to and from work in factories among a cacophony of churning machinery and under soot-belching smokestacks. Downtown Mystic, where upscale housing, shops and restaurants now abound, was once full of pubs, small groceries, hardware stores and an opera house.

Even familiar contemporary landmarks built long ago have changed. The iconic Mystic drawbridge is one example. Ferries transported people and animals across the river beginning in the 1600s. In 1818, the Connecticut General Assembly was petitioned to bridge the river, and the first bridge—a wood one—was financed and built by private developers and investors. Travelers paid a toll to cross. That bridge was rebuilt in 1830 and finally became a public entity when purchased by the towns of Groton and Stonington in 1854. The first iron bridge across the river was built in 1866 then later strengthened to carry trolleys across. The bascule bridge that is now a favorite landmark finally opened in 1922.

Looking east in downtown Mystic at the Mystic River drawbridge construction in the 1920s. *Courtesy Mystic River Historical Society Inc., Mystic, Connecticut.*

Laborers work to construct the Mystic River drawbridge in the 1920s. *Courtesy Mystic River Historical Society Inc., Mystic, Connecticut.*

Lodging by the Sea

When the Providence and Stonington Railroad opened in 1837, it was the state's first railroad. It revolutionized travel. Travelers between New York City and Providence rode on steamships through Long Island Sound and then traveled by train between Stonington and Providence. Stonington transformed from a sleepy seaside village to a bustling East Coast transportation center. But it was the building of an elegant hotel named the Wadawanuck House that helped make Stonington a destination for travelers and vacationers for many decades both before and after the Civil War. The sprawling hotel occupied what is now the quiet, leafy Wadawanuck Square, home to the Stonington Free Library. The hotel also housed an early women's college.

Benjamin Palmer built the hotel at the same time that the Providence and Stonington Railroad was being planned and constructed. When the railroad line opened on November 10, 1837, the hotel hosted a celebratory banquet that "was spoken of for many a day," according to a *Stonington Mirror* article published in 1930, long after the hotel was demolished.

Emma W. Palmer also talked about the hotel in an address she gave to the local historical society in 1906. In the written manuscript of her speech, she recalled the hotel being the center of village social entertainment for years. While most were attracted to Stonington in the summer months, she wrote about fond memories of the hotel's many wintertime activities, including sleighing parties and winter balls. In the late 1840s, the hotel housed a bowling alley and a billiards room and for at least one night hosted President John Tyler. By the early 1850s, it was a popular center for ladies' swim lessons and a frequent wedding destination for Rhode Island couples seeking to avoid the stricter marriage laws in the nearby Ocean State.

A June 24, 1850 article in the *Hartford Courant* called the Wadawanuck "one of the most delightful retreats in New England during the warm season." The article reported:

> *A correspondent for* The New York Express *who has been enjoying the healthful and invigorating sea breeze of Stonington, thinks it one of the most perfect places as a summer resort ever visited. The salt water fishing is rarely equaled and there are fine trout ponds in the vicinity. There are excellent accommodations for bathing and those who wish to enjoy the excitement of surf bathing, will find it to perfection at Watch Hill,*

Railroad Yard and Steam Boat Docks, Stonington, Conn.

Stonington became a major transportation center after the 1837 completion of the railroad to Providence, Rhode Island. *Rhode Island News Company postcard, courtesy Mystic Seaport Museum.*

about twenty minutes sail from Stonington. There is daily communication between Hartford and Stonington via the Willimantic Rail Roads [sic] *and steamboat from New London.*

While the Wadawanuck House seems to have remained popular through the years with both local residents and travelers, as a business it apparently was not that lucrative. It changed both ownership and managers numerous times. By the late 1850s, it temporarily ceased operating as a hotel and became a women's college, albeit a short-lived one.

The college opened in the 1857–58 academic year and attracted about sixty resident students, along with another one hundred locals as day scholars. Young ladies came from as far away as New York City, Michigan and New Jersey. In a November 1978 edition of the Stonington Historical Society's newsletter *Historical Footnotes*, Minor Myers Jr. called the Wadawanuck Young Ladies Institute the state's first women's college.

At that time, Myers was a Connecticut College professor, but he later went on to become president of Illinois Wesleyan University.

Wadawanuck was a true college and not a high school or an advanced seminary, Myers wrote. Students graduated knowing Latin and a modern foreign language. They also studied grammar, rhetoric, writing, critical reading, oil painting, drawing, music and the legal rights of women.

An 1859 broadside advertisement promoted the school, saying it offered easy access and a safe resort for educational purposes and featured airy hallways and a piazza that allowed for outdoor exercise in all weather. The Reverend H.A. Sackett attested in the advertisement that the school paid particular regard "to the cultivation of morals, manners and correct personal habits."

The preferences and strict racial hierarchy and prejudices of the era are illustrated in a 1934 *Stonington Mirror* article recalling a "Wadawanuck female college Christmas" of the early 1860s. Typical of the day, entertainment centered on speaking and the mostly lost art of tableaux, which were static

Large elegantly furnished rooms, salubrity of climate unequaled; a place for real solid comfort, rest and recreation. Send for illustrated circular, plan of rooms, etc.

HOTEL WADAWANUCK,
STONINGTON, CONN.

The Wadawanuck hotel opened in 1837, the same year the railroad was completed in Stonington. The Stonington Free Library is now located on the square where the hotel stood. *Courtesy collection of the Stonington Historical Society.*

scenes or living pictures staged by the students. They depicted well-known historic events, scenes from literature and other displays. The article notes a particular tableau, "Our Picture," presented by Lena Denison, Lucy Babcock and Nellie Babcock. It was loudly applauded, and the audience asked for more. Instead of re-creating the same tableau, however, the young ladies apparently decided to play a joke on the audience, one that seems crude and racist today but was acceptable at the time. The article notes: "The curtain slowly drawn—we see the same lady holding the frame, but ugh! Instead of the same face in the frame, we behold a little darky!"

While it's not clear why the college closed in 1862 after just five years of operation, an article about it in the *Stonington Mirror* in 1896 postulated that the Civil War, and the societal upheaval it brought, might have played a role in its demise. The writer also notes that the "principal became weary perhaps of keeping the village boys from the flock of girlhood beauty."

The college's closing ended one chapter in the building's life, but another soon began as the Wadawanuck House was again converted to its original use as a hotel. By most accounts, the hotel's heyday was in the 1870s.

It was during that era when an advertisement in *Walling's Route and City Guides—Stonington Line* dubbed the destination a "first class family hotel" featuring bathing, fishing, driving and sailing. Further, the ad called it "one of the most delightful resorts for summer recreation to be found upon the coast."

An April 18, 1930 *Stonington Mirror* obituary for a Mrs. William Reynolds Brown of New York City noted that she often recalled staying with her family at the hotel when it "was in all its glory." She talked about walking a mile via fourteen trips around the hotel's piazza.

In August 1875, the *Hartford Courant* reported: "The Wadawanuck House is charmingly situated and as a summer resort is not excelled in many respects by many in New England. There may be other resorts where the air is just as sweet and exhilarating—and I hope there are, and many—but I do not know of them." After discussing the superior qualities of the hotel's proprietors and noting that the vicinity abounds in beautiful landscape and architecture, the writer continues: "At night at least a dozen sparkling lighthouses may be seen from the cupola of the Wadawanuck. In fact, there are few places where better glimpses of the briny deep can be had than at Stonington."

Just a few years later, cards advertising the hotel noted its large, airy rooms, excellent beds and superior dining featuring local fresh vegetables and pure milk. "All of the comforts of a first-class family hotel, *perfectly free*

Guests of the Wadawanuck House could take a ferry from Stonington to the popular summer resort of Watch Hill, Rhode Island. *Courtesy Stonington Historical Society, Maurice LaGrua Photograph Collection.*

from malaria." All this enjoyment could be had for about $3 a day or between $12 and $20 a week. In 2020 terms, $12 would be nearly $310, a rate that would be an incredible bargain for a week's vacation in 2020.

Despite its popularity, the Wadawanuck closed for good some time around 1890. The character of Stonington village was quickly changing. Stonington's existence as a main transportation center was in steep decline as completion of a railroad bridge over the Thames River to the west changed train routes. Railroads merged, and the Stonington steamship lines soon ceased running.

Commercial activity on the hotel site ended when the Wadawanuck was demolished in 1893 to make way for a new public library, the Stonington Free Library, which remains today. All that's left of the once sizable hotel is the name of the square—Wadawanuck, a Native American word of uncertain meaning.

EDUCATION FOR THE DEAF

High on a hill overlooking the Mystic River about two miles north of downtown Mystic, a group of abandoned brick buildings is all that remains of a historically significant school that operated there for more than a century. (There is currently talk of redeveloping this property.) Mystic Oral School, originally called the Whipple Home School for Deaf Mutes, survived periods of mismanagement, intense fights about the most appropriate methods by which to teach deaf students and repeated threats of public funding losses. The school finally closed in 1980, a victim of both its high cost of operations and a dwindling student population caused by contemporary viewpoints that frowned on education that isolated children with distinct needs.

While the school had a rather inauspicious end, for decades its dedicated advocates saw it as a progressive school that provided opportunities for the deaf at a time when many of those with special physical, emotional or mental health needs were shunned.

Even when education for the deaf was in its infancy in the early nineteenth century, there were two distinct schools of thought about the most appropriate method of instruction and communication. The American School in Hartford, organized in 1815 and still in operation as the American School for the Deaf in West Hartford, adhered to a so-called manual or signing system. Today, American Sign Language is the primary method of communication among the deaf and viewed as a distinct language.

Others, however, once gravitated to the oral method, which emphasized lip reading and vocal communication. Jonathan Whipple, a Rogerene Quaker who was a founder of the local branch of the Universal Peace Union and who lived in Quakertown, part of what is now the town of Ledyard that is located just a short distance from Mystic, adopted this oral method when seeking to educate his deaf son, Enoch. Jonathan had noticed that his son learned to read lips, leading father and son to develop a communication system with each other. Jonathan realized that every word had an accompanying distinct mouth shape that could be imitated by the hearing impaired, allowing them to learn to speak. This so inspired Jonathan's grandson Zerah C. Whipple that in 1869, he established the Whipple Home School for Deaf Mutes in an old farmhouse on Colonel Ledyard Highway in Quakertown.

Although it's likely because of the isolated nature of the Rogerenes that Jonathan Whipple may not have fully understood his contribution to education for the deaf, in a March 1897 address to the Committee on Humane Institutions in Hartford, Alexander Graham Bell said,

"To Jonathan Whipple of Mystic belongs the honors of having first demonstrated auricular development in the deaf; and though the importance of the discovery was not understood or appreciated at the time—even by himself—we know it now."

In 1872, the school began receiving state aid to provide education for its students. Also around this same time, the school relocated from its humble Ledyard farmhouse to a larger structure at the school's longtime Mystic site. By 1885, after Zerah's death, the school was sold out of the Whipple family's control and entered a period marked by intense criticism and punctuated by a battle between it and the American School for scarce state dollars. Officials at the oral school were accused of mismanagement that led to indebtedness and possibly a degradation of students' living conditions.

While a booklet detailing the school's history praises progress made under the direction of Dr. Clara M.H. McGuigan, who took control around 1895, newspaper articles from that era paint a different picture.

In a *Hartford Courant* article published on April 2, 1897, under the headline "Mystic Oral School: State Board of Charities Condemns It," members of the board said their problems with the school had nothing to do with the dispute over the most appropriate method by which to educate deaf students but rather focused on what they considered poor living conditions at the school.

One board member said that when she visited the Mystic facility she found it rundown and lacking fire escapes. "The school is in a cheerless spot and the children are not taught any trade," the board member noted. The board also focused on the school's management under McGuigan's direction. They noted that McGuigan's mother, who was the former school principal, was in hiding and was believed to have embezzled school money. McGuigan herself was seldom at the site, the board charged.

An even more scathing opinion article from this same era was published in a local newspaper: "The state of Connecticut is being robbed in a number of ways but there probably never was such a bare-faced assault on the public money as has been made by the management of the Whipple home for the deaf at Mystic." The article continued, "The building is a ramshackle affair and there are no conveniences whatever for children who are inmates."

The article also accuses McGuigan's mother of embezzling $10,000 of state funds and bilking the state further by billing it for more students than actually were being schooled. Also noting that McGuigan was a resident of Philadelphia who visited Mystic only about once each month, the article contended that both she and her mother were poor stewards for the school.

A school for the deaf operated in this Mystic house from the early 1870s. A later iteration on the same site was long called the Mystic Oral School. *Courtesy Mystic River Historical Society Inc., Mystic, Connecticut.*

Despite this fight over state aid to the school, McGuigan remained in control in Mystic until 1921. During that period, not only did the state continue to give the school aid, but it also actually purchased the school, which had been renamed Mystic Oral School. In the 1920s and 1930s, the school expanded. It added dormitories, a superintendent's home, increased classroom space and an administration building. It also withstood efforts around 1940 to merge it with the American School for the Deaf.

By 1975, passage of the Federal Education of All Handicapped Children Act marked the beginning of the end for Mystic Oral School. Diseases such as rubella and measles that previously led to spikes of childhood deafness were in decline. A continuing debate about the efficacy of the oral method of teaching the hearing impaired, and a general trend toward integrating children with a variety of special needs into regular classrooms, combined to force the school's closure.

With staff outnumbering students ninety-two to sixty-seven and operating expenses of about $21,000 per student, the Mystic Oral School was preparing to close, the *New York Times* reported on April 14, 1980. After the school's closure, the facility was repurposed as a school for developmentally disabled students. That school closed in 2011. More than a century of progressive and sometimes controversial education was over.

Caring for the Poorest Residents

By the time Ernie Dickson was eighteen, he had already lived in more than six places. Two homes were ramshackle dwellings on the banks of the Mystic River that flooded at each high tide, and two were foster homes at which he was little more than a farmhand. One was a state-run institution for children in Norwich. Just after his eighteenth birthday in 1937, when Stonington and the rest of the country was still struggling through the Great Depression, he was forced to live in a place he said frightened him to the core—Stonington's Town Farm.

"This was one of the few times I really broke down. I was scared to death there," Dickson recalled in a 2001 interview focusing on his rise from poverty. "I was the only young person there."

In the days before Social Security, public disability payments, government-subsidized housing and state-assisted nutrition programs, many towns in New England operated almshouses as shelters of last resort for the destitute. In small towns and rural areas, including Stonington, municipally supported almshouses often were farms where residents worked planting, weeding and harvesting or helping care for livestock. Stonington's Town Farm was located on Wheeler Road.

While life was arguably tougher for all at a time when health care was rudimentary by contemporary standards and most people made livings via hard physical labor, life was especially cruel for the poor. Dickson's determination to get an education and rise out of his difficult early circumstances to become a notable school administrator is all the more remarkable given the general circumstances of the era in which he lived.

Dickson's sad early circumstances were not unique, however. In Stonington, almshouse records were kept in an oversized bound ledger now located at the Stonington Historical Society's Richard W. Woolworth Library and Research Center. Beginning when the farm opened in 1868 and until it closed in 1955, the farm keepers painstakingly recorded the names, ages, dates of admission and something of the circumstances of each person who came into their care. The farm's first resident, for example, was a sixty-two-year-old white male who was a native of Stonington. He was temperate, according to the information recorded, but also suffered "partial insanity." He lived at the farm for more than thirty years. His death was recorded there in January 1896.

Others were logged in as being lame, infirm, insane, crippled, destitute, blind or simply poor. Some suffered the impacts of old age. One was recorded as having blood poisoning. During the Depression years, the ledger told the stories of those worst hit by the poor financial times. Residents came to the farm as "down and out," "destitute," on "hard times" or having "no work."

Dickson, who later served as principal at three of Stonington's public schools before retiring in 1983, ended up at the Town Farm because he grew up poor and his mother died when he was just eleven years old. He was born in 1919 on Mason's Island, which in the early years of the twentieth century was a workaday place whose residents would likely be unable to fathom the island's current status as a place of sprawling, upscale houses. The Dickson family—six children and two parents—twice packed all of their worldly belongings into a rowboat and moved to different spots on the Mystic waterfront.

"We lived right on the Mystic River, but it was so polluted then, no one who had money wanted to live there," Dickson recalled in the interview recounting his early life. "I remember the toilets would flow right into the river. They'd build them out over the water like that. We'd swim there and eat the fish from there."

One place Dickson lived was in the section of Mystic known as Fort Rachel, a spot that played a role in staving off the British during the War of 1812. By the early twentieth century, the place was also known as Bogue's Alley or Bogue Town, a neighborhood some Mystic residents long described as being home to the devil himself. In 1919, Helen May Clarke of Mystic was just shy of ten years old when she described the area in her diary.

"Summer people think Bogue Town and the docks very quaint and of course they do have local color as the artists say," she wrote in August that year. "Bogue Town is dirty but I like it. It smells of tar and rope and paint and drying nets, besides the salt from the river and a good big whiff of fish thrown in. It is one of my favorite smells. There are others underneath, more like stinks, because the [residents] are not very sanitary." She also wrote of Water Street, which led into Fort Rachel and was known to locals as Rotten Row: "Rotten Row is not a nice place on account of the dirty houses along it. They have a very bad smell on hot summer nights. It is a sort of interesting stink."

In reality, the neighborhood many locals shunned or looked down on was occupied by poor residents forced to live in substandard housing because it was all they could afford. Dickson's father worked wherever he could find someone willing to hire him, including in local shipyards and as an itinerant carpenter. At night, he often caught eels in the Mystic River, and the family survived on fried eels, local clams and wild blueberries. When Dickson's mother died, leaving six children under the age of twelve, his father could not manage the family on his own. The children were taken to live at the New London County Temporary Home, a facility for destitute children located in Norwich, where Dickson recalled he tasted peanut butter for the first time and also got to go camping.

"I was unable to finish school that year because I was so undernourished," Dickson said of his first year at the state facility.

After about two years in the children's home, however, the Dickson children were healthy enough to be sent to foster care. Many foster families at the time were seeking strong children to help with farm and household chores. Dickson recalled living with families who had many strict rules. He worked daily milking cows and in the barns and fields. He also walked five miles each way to and from school.

When he turned eighteen, the state's financial responsibility for him ended. He was on his own. With no place to go, he headed back to Mystic, where he slept outdoors, in friends' attics or in hammocks on porches until the day a friend said Dickson needed to go to the Town Farm to live.

Dickson remembered the bedrooms at the farm as dark and tiny. They were sparsely furnished with a narrow metal-framed bed, a chair and a nightstand. The elderly men who made up most of the farm's residents were thrilled to see a young man and frequently sought him out for conversation. Still, for a teenager who preferred being with young people, the affable elderly residents, some of whom were alcoholics or suffering from mental health challenges, seemed frightening. The farm felt like a foreboding place. The couple who ran the farm took pity on Dickson. He didn't do farmwork and was allowed to take his meals with one other younger resident in the kitchen, away from the other residents.

Because the town paid to operate the farm and provided for the residents' basic needs, the town's selectmen tried to convince Dickson to leave the farm and join the Civilian Conservation Corps, the Depression-era program through which many young men were put to work planting trees, clearing trails and building recreational facilities in parks and campgrounds. Dickson, however, was determined to finish high school and even dreamed of going to college. He attended his senior year of high school as a resident of the almshouse, graduating from Stonington High School, then located in the borough, in 1938. He later served in the military and completed college. His was a remarkable journey, from the outer margins of a society that viewed him and others like him as a burden, to a position of great respect and responsibility in the same community.

The Town Farm continued to operate as housing of last resort for the most needy town residents until 1955. The building that housed part of the farm still stands. It is now the Pequot Golf Club's clubhouse. A wing of unused almshouse rooms—each about eight feet by ten feet with tiny windows and a sloped ceiling—still exists on the second floor.

4
IMMIGRANTS SHAPE THE COMMUNITY

Anthony Squadrito was among a wave of some five million Italian immigrants who came to America between 1880 and 1920. Hailing from a village near Messina, Sicily, Squadrito found his way to Stonington, where he worked as a barber and had a popular band.

He charmed many local ladies with his dark good looks and enchanting singing voice. One day, as he sang to a maid in a Stonington household, he also caught the eyes and ears of her boss, the widow of sea captain Thomas Burtch. Harriet Burtch was sixty-six and Squadrito just twenty-five when the two eloped shortly thereafter and were married by a Catholic priest in Boston. The marriage took place on June 10, 1903. While the union scandalized Stonington society, Squadrito, his brothers and their descendants became well known and respected as barbers in Stonington, Mystic and Noank.

The public splash made by Squadrito is far from the typical immigrant story. Most who found their way to Stonington and Mystic from foreign shores worked long days in relative obscurity in factories and quarries, as fishermen or as laborers building roads or laying railroad and trolley tracks. Railroad officials in the 1830s often headed to Boston, where they recruited Irish workers directly from immigrant ships. Newspapers reported Italian workers camping out near Wequetequock while constructing trolley lines through town at the turn of the twentieth century.

Irish and Portuguese fishermen from the Azores were among the town's earliest waves of immigrants. Italians, Poles, English, French Canadians, Germans and others followed. At first, most immigrants remained segregated

Mills lined both sides of the Pawcatuck River at Stillmanville in the early 1900s. Many new immigrants found work in the mills. *Courtesy Westerly Library & Wilcox Park.*

from Yankee residents with longer histories in the area. Each immigrant group also remained segregated from other new arrivals. The Irish and Italians in Pawcatuck, for example, settled near one another and attended the same church but sat on separate sides of the aisle at Mass, even well into the mid-twentieth century.

Most immigrants were largely ignored by the local press unless they committed a crime, died in an unusual fashion or seemed like local oddities. One story that did make it into the local newspapers, for example, focused on an Irish immigrant named Dennis Coleman, a native of County Longford who lived with his family on Morgan Street, Pawcatuck, in the shadow of St. Michael's Church. He died in a well explosion when a dynamite charge detonated prematurely. An article in the *Narragansett Weekly* on October 3, 1872, included some colorful information in the account of his funeral: "The Ancient Order of Hibernians, accompanied by the Westerly Brass Band attended the funeral."

A *Hartford Courant* article published on December 23, 1912, under the headline "Chinaman Came to Stonington in 1859" is another example. The article speculates whether a man who had died and was identified by the writer only as Garry was the first Chinese man to live in town.

A Life at Sea

When he was interviewed in 1979 for a book about the Stonington fishing community published by the Mystic Seaport, Tim Medeiros recalled the strength of the ties binding his family to that livelihood. He also recognized, however, that many of the fishing community's women endured unique challenges.

"Of course, my mother didn't like it too much," he said about the lifestyle. "She was brought up in the tough days down there, when most of the guys, when they came in they went to the local pubs. I guess there used to be about nine pubs in Stonington, and I think they spent most of their time and money there."

Commercial fishing has long been an integral part of the Borough of Stonington's identity. Repeatedly rated as one of the most dangerous professions, fishing requires its practitioners to spend long periods at sea exposed to the harshest of conditions. While the profession continues to be dominated by males, the females connected to fishing—either heading to sea themselves or as the wives, daughters, sisters and loved ones of males who go to sea—also endure significant, if not always appreciated, hardships.

In a 1993 series of oral history interviews conducted by the Mystic Seaport, along with information included in the earlier Seaport book titled *Fishing Out of Stonington*, edited by Fred Calabretta, women recall the stresses of being a member of a fishing family. They lived in dirty, damp and crude conditions near the Stonington docks beginning in the middle of the nineteenth century. They were largely shut out of the male-dominated world. They sometimes experienced excruciating emotional pain awaiting the return of boats reported missing. Some ultimately received bad news about a loved one's fate. Women also were confined to homes with large numbers of small children while husbands were at sea. They rose in predawn hours to see their husbands off to work. They struggled to manage a large household on sometimes unpredictable wages.

On the positive side, the bonds among Stonington fishing families were strong. Many families share a common religion and culture, hailing from the Azores. The men on the various boats looked out for one another. Village merchants were friendly and accommodating. Families pulled together in both bad times and good and sought solace in their traditions.

The long title of a biographical short story written by Mary Madeira and published in the August 1973 edition of the Stonington Historical Society newsletter sums up the lifestyle this way: "This is a story of young love and marriage; babies and bills; heartbreak and happiness; the story of a fisherman's incredible courage in times of disaster." Madeira's story focused largely on the life of her sister Connie and her brother-in-law Manuel. He immigrated to Stonington from the Azores in 1902.

Well before Manuel Madeira joined other Portuguese fishing families in Stonington, the village's geography tied it to the sea. Called Long Point in the early years of European settlement, it was home to some five hundred English transplants by the mid-eighteenth century, and many of those were heading to sea in pursuit of fish and, later, whales and seals.

The number of Stonington fishermen rose and fell through the years, depending on the demand for seafood, financial conditions, laws and regulations. Early in the nineteenth century, numbers increased after the government offered a bounty to any active cod fisherman who fished at least four months a year. Just after the War of 1812, Stonington had a fleet of more than a dozen vessels and was landing tens of thousands of pounds of salt cod. Stonington fishermen were supplying seafood to both New York City and Boston.

When the government bounty ended just after the Civil War, commercial fishing decreased, then rebounded near the turn of the twentieth century. By 1893, nearly fifty Stonington fishing vessels bringing catches of mostly cod and haddock employed more than 260 men. The number of boats continued to stand at about fifty through the Great Depression. By 1950, there were several hundred Stonington fishermen, about half of whom were of Portuguese descent.

The first Portuguese immigrants began to make their way across the Atlantic to Stonington village in the mid-1800s. Frank G. Sylvia, who was born in the Azores in 1824, was among the first Portuguese immigrants to Stonington. He settled on a farm outside the village. Many others of his countrymen who came to Stonington instead chose a life at sea.

As is typical of new immigrants, life was not easy for these families at first. The housing many lived in near the water's edge at the south end of the borough was cold, dark, damp and, in a word, miserable. "Manuel and Connie's apartment was on the first floor," Mary Madeira wrote in the biographical piece, referring to the couple's home in 1908. "Being near the water, it was very cold and damp. The room they slept in was on the north side of the house. During the winter months, she would hang newspapers on the walls and windows to absorb the moisture. The large kitchen stove burned wood during the day, and coal at night."

Without central heating, the Madeiras used flannel-wrapped, fire-heated bricks to keep their bed warm. One young child slept between them to help the youngster stay warm. The baby was wrapped in extra layers in his nearby cradle. When a blizzard in February 1908 blew icy winds through the house and dumped two feet of snow on the village, the couple's efforts to fight the elements failed.

"I remember so well, Connie putting a woolen cap and mittens on baby Joe and an extra blanket over him in the cradle," Mary Madeira wrote. Mary's father's alarm clock rang at 4:00 a.m. The family soon heard a commotion from her sister's apartment below them. "Suddenly we heard Connie screaming hysterically from downstairs. Dad ran down and Mother got up and ran after him. I was in a daze, thinking it was a fire, and followed them. There was Connie with baby Joe dead in her arms."

The weather prevented the family from fetching the doctor to their home until about 8:00 a.m. When the physician examined the infant, he said the baby died of exposure. "He looked around and noticed the windows and walls covered with newspapers and said, 'It's a wonder you people haven't died of pneumonia with this dampness.'" The doctor advised the couple to move before having more children, not seeming to recognize that the family lived where they could afford to.

In later years, housing conditions improved as basic systems such as central heating became more common, but the inherent danger of commercial fishing continued to make for some distressing, even heartbreaking, times for women who had loved ones at sea.

Ann M. Rita, who was interviewed for the seaport's oral history project, recalled life as both the daughter and wife of fishermen. Her father worked a full-time night shift at Electric Boat and headed out from the docks on his lobster boat each morning to support his family of seven children. Later, as a young wife, she recalled the day she went to the dock with her two-year-old son in tow to meet her husband after a day of fishing. Mother and son instead were greeted by the sight of the fishing boat *Rosemary R* ablaze. Although she learned the men aboard were safe, the scene was a shock.

Doris Berg, also interviewed by the seaport, recalled driving her husband to work at the Stonington docks at 2:00 a.m. daily. The docks were noisy and smelly, she said, and women were not allowed near the boats because of the foul language used there.

Those whose husbands did not return to port daily also faced isolation. Betty Fellows said her husband was often at sea for ten days or more at a time. Her story about struggling to raise young children on her own is included in the Mystic Seaport book about Stonington fishing. When her oldest was just a kindergartener, she recalled that the child was stricken with both measles and chickenpox. Soon, all her children were sick. "For six weeks, I didn't stick my nose out the door, except to hang clothes," she said. "I called my mother in tears." She begged her mother to watch the children for just a few minutes so she could take a brief walk to clear her head.

Today, a small commercial fishing fleet, one of the state's last, remains a vital part of Stonington Borough. While many fishermen moved out of the borough in the second half of the twentieth century as property values and taxes there increased along with demand for village houses by wealthy out-of-staters, fishing boats continue to launch from the town dock there. Fishermen still sell their catches at the docks or at local farmers markets, gather at the Portuguese Holy Ghost Society and mark the Blessing of the Fleet each July.

At the end of the town dock, where steamboats once docked, a fishermen's memorial dedicated on July 8, 1979, lists the names of forty-one Stonington fishermen who died at sea. Not listed on the memorial are the names of the women—the wives, mothers and daughters—who shared in this ultimate sacrifice.

IRISH PRESENCE

In the 1920s, parades were key community events in Stonington's easternmost village of Pawcatuck. Among the floats, bands and dignitaries marching, the Boy Scout troops in full regalia were an important and popular contingent.

In 1920, more than sixty years after St. Michael the Archangel Roman Catholic Church was built to serve those who flocked here seeking a better life, the sting of religious bigotry was still being felt. That year, the church formed a Boy Scout troop, and more than fifty neighborhood boys soon became Scouts. The boys were eager to show off their uniforms and be cheered on by well-wishers along a parade route. So, when a parade was being planned, Father John J. Keane and George Chapman, the Scout leaders, submitted the troop's application. They began preparing the boys to march.

The men soon were surprised, however, to receive notice that their request to participate was denied. It must be some mistake, they thought, perhaps a clerical error. They resubmitted the application. Again, denied.

Despite repeated requests, the troop continued to be barred from the parade. Then reality dawned on the Scout leaders—this was the latest example of anti-Catholic sentiment against the parishioners of Pawcatuck by those in power locally. St. Michael, and by extension its many Irish immigrant parishioners, had not been wholeheartedly welcomed into the village. Even more than a half century since the church was established in the 1850s, those of Irish ancestry still tended to socialize mainly with other Irish, because the larger community did not fully embrace them and their Catholic religion. The attitude didn't change even as many in their ranks became wealthier and opened prominent local businesses.

At the time St. Michael was established, anti-Catholic Know Nothingism was at its zenith in the United States. Besides being anti-Catholic, Know Nothings were anti-immigrant and anti-alcohol. Many Americans who did not embrace the extremism of the Know Nothings still were wary and fearful of the increasing number of immigrants coming into the country.

In 1855, Connecticut, Rhode Island and Massachusetts all elected governors from the American Party, the Know Nothings' formal title. State legislatures also had large contingents of Know Nothings in their ranks. In Rhode Island, one legislator from Pawcatuck's sister town of Westerly, just over the state border, joined with a colleague to submit a bill to require immigrants to reside in the United States for twenty-one years before becoming eligible to vote. They feared that the pope and Catholicism would overtake the U.S. government.

By the time Know Nothingism was on the rise, Irish immigrants had lived in Stonington for more than two decades. Unskilled Irish workers were first recruited and brought to Stonington Borough to work on constructing the railroad in the 1830s. George Washington Whistler, father of the painter James Whistler and a preeminent engineer overseeing the rail line construction, recruited fresh-off-the-boat Irish immigrants in Providence. By the 1840s and 1850s, however, the potato famine was decimating Ireland and the exodus from that country had reached meteoric proportions. The famine claimed one million lives and, before it ended in 1852, pushed another million to leave their homeland. The Irish drawn to Pawcatuck found jobs in manufacturing and quarrying. By the late 1800s, they were sometimes called the "tin dinner pail brigades," because they thronged the Pawcatuck streets each morning and evening on their way to and from the mills and quarries. In the early days, they practiced their faith with outdoor Masses said by an itinerant priest from Hartford. These took place in a wooded grove off Morgan Street, historian Larry O'Keefe writes in *Historic Stonington*, a publication of the Stonington Historical Society.

During this population surge, George Downer laid out one of Pawcatuck's first subdivisions. The neighborhood was planned for land once owned by Downer's father-in-law, Dr. William Robinson, who had died in 1845. The Irish became familiar with Downer as the affable man eager to sell them building lots in the neighborhood that came to be called Downerville, a name it retains today.

Most of the local population was not as eager as Downer to have the Irish in their midst, however. When the Diocese of Hartford sought to build St. Michael in Pawcatuck, the task was achieved only after some convoluted land transactions made necessary by a refusal among landowners to sell to the Irish.

Bishop Francis P. McFarland bought a 1.5-acre lot on the south side of Liberty Street for $250 in 1859 from a noted local development firm, the C. Maxson Company. That transaction was the first and last simple diocesan land purchase. After the church was constructed, in 1862, the diocese needed more land for a rectory and sought to purchase another parcel from a prominent local landowner named Abby Lewis. The church secured the land, however, only after a businessman named Richard F. Loper purchased it and then traded it to the diocese for other land he wanted in the Borough of Stonington. The borough property Loper sought had been owned by St. Mary Church. Loper was one of Stonington's most prominent citizens, and his huge mansion long stood near Wadawanuck Square, at the site of the current post office.

After another decade passed, St. Michael was again in the market for land. The parish wanted to establish a Catholic school. A perfect site was located diagonally across Liberty Street from the church. The property was owned by William C. Maxson, a member of the family who ran the C. Maxson Company, which sold the original church parcel to the diocese. Maxson was not eager for St. Michael to expand, however, although he apparently harbored no ill will against individual immigrants. He sold his land to Thomas Bennett, an Irish immigrant who was superintendent at a local granite quarry.

Bennett didn't want the property for himself. He bought the house and land from Maxson one day and, for the same price, sold it to the parish the next day.

In 1890, the parish again used an intermediary to buy more land on which to expand its school. Developers Pendleton & Hall owned the tract just across Liberty Street from the church. Michael Higgins, a parishioner, bought the land and again resold it to the parish for an identical price.

The sons of many of Pawcatuck's Irish immigrants joined St. Michael's Boy Scout troop in the 1920s. *Courtesy Larry O'Keefe, James Donahue Collection.*

Workers at Pawcatuck's Clark thread mill, shown at left, and other local factories, used this pedestrian bridge over the Pawcatuck River to commute in the early 1900s. *Courtesy Westerly Library & Wilcox Park.*

St. Michael's Church in Pawcatuck also had a fife and drum corps in the 1920s. *Courtesy Larry O'Keefe, James Donahue Collection.*

Against this backdrop, and recalling that anti–Irish Catholic sentiment persisted even to 1960, when John F. Kennedy ran for president, it becomes less surprising that in 1920 such prejudice remained in Pawcatuck. By this time, the many Irish immigrants also had been joined by a flood of Italian immigrants, who also were Catholic.

Perhaps motivated by the creative maneuvering used in the land acquisition, Father Keane refused to accept his Scouts' rejection from the parade. He told the boys to dress in their uniforms and gather in front of the church on parade day. He handed out American flags and topped off his own outfit with a tall silk hat. A professional photographer snapped the troop's picture in front of the church, and they then marched down Liberty Street and across the Pawcatuck River into Westerly. There, they awaited the parade's arrival. When the Boy Scout division approached, Father Keane waved his top hat, leading his boys into the parade. The parade's division chief tried to extricate the intruders, but the public cheered and clapped for the boys until they were allowed to remain. They marched the rest of the route with the other local Scouts.

It would be the last time a parade committee tried to prevent the Catholic Scout troop from participating in a local parade.

A New Life in a New Place

By the third quarter of the nineteenth century, Mystic's community leaders were becoming concerned about the stagnating local economy. They searched for a way to diversify the area's economy, which until that time was almost totally dependent on shipbuilding and other seafaring businesses. With textile manufacturing already a strong industry in eastern Connecticut, they worked to lure a large textile manufacturer to the village.

It took time, but in 1897, the Mystic Industrial Company was incorporated, and $22,000 (about $682,000 in 2020) was raised to bring a European manufacturer to town. It wouldn't be just any type of mill. Local leaders were determined to have a German velvet mill in Mystic, much like the Wimpfheimer velvet factory established in 1892 in Stonington village. Elias Williams donated two acres on the east bank of the Mystic River on what is now Route 27, also known as Greenmanville Avenue, as a factory site.

Besides these local incentives, the Tariff Act of 1890 (also called the McKinley Tariff) made imported goods more expensive and the establishment of domestic industries attractive, resulting in many more domestic manufacturers. By 1898, the Rossie Velvet Company mill was built and began operations.

As the establishment of the Rossie mill illustrates, industrialization in the nineteenth and early twentieth centuries entailed more than building a factory. It often meant relocating an entire community of immigrants as workers. Successfully luring workers might require promising them more than jobs. It often included offering conveniently located housing, recreational facilities, religious institutions and social opportunities.

Traveling across an ocean and adjusting to foreign customs, languages, schools and even unfamiliar weather could be intimidating to those making the often perilous journey. But they weren't the only ones who had to come to grips with a new reality. The infusion of foreign-born, often non-English-speaking residents to a small town populated predominantly by Connecticut Yankees also required some adjustments on the part of the host community. Immigrants, then as now, were not universally embraced in the United States, and the type of mass migrations experienced following the Irish Potato Famine and other political and social upheavals in Europe were just beginning. The process was not always smooth.

Despite the challenges, many immigrants did come to power the mills of Stonington and Mystic. They were part of a larger transformation as many small New England towns went from seafaring and agricultural communities to bustling centers of industry that were hubs of innovation in a fast-changing world. In Mystic and Stonington, just as in communities throughout the state and the Northeast, it was immigrant men, women and children who provided the bodies and the brawn to produce thread, velvet, woolen goods and other products. In fact, so many immigrants came to power Connecticut's industry in the late nineteenth and early twentieth centuries that they forever changed the state. While three-quarters of Connecticut's residents were American born in 1870, only 35 percent were by World War I.

Many Germans came to work in Stonington's velvet mills because they had been skilled in the industry in Germany. English were lured to provide the labor force at the Clark thread mill in Pawcatuck, Polish to work at the Old Mystic mills and Italian laborers for the quarries.

Immigrants also touched off a building boom. A December 30, 1905 article in the *Hartford Courant* was published under the headline "Building Boom Strikes Mystic; Village Making the Biggest Growth in Its History; Velvet and Woolen Mills Contribute to Its Prosperity." The article notes that the Rossie mill employed about 350 people and was building an addition. This, together with expansions at other mills, spurred construction of more than twenty-five new houses.

While news of the establishment of the factories and the economic boost they produced was well documented, the same cannot be said of the personal stories of the early industrial workers. The immigrants were consumed by their efforts to survive and exhausted by working an average of fifty-three hours a week, according to figures from the Bureau of Labor Statistics. This left scarce time to compile personal journals and pensive writings that would tell their stories to future generations.

Immigrants were mentioned in news articles only rarely. Exceptions included when immigrant workers were involved in industrial accidents. In the July 12, 1901 edition of the *Hartford Courant*, one such article noted: "Caught in Shafting; A Mill Hand's Arm Torn Off at the Elbow." The accident occurred at Stonington Borough's Atwood-Morrison factory.

"Manuel Capella, a Portuguese, employed at the Atwood-Morrison silk machine factory, was caught in the shafting there today and received injuries which will probably prove fatal. The man's arm was torn off at the elbow," the article reported, noting that Capella was adjusting a belt on machinery when the ladder he was on collapsed, sending him into the still-moving equipment. He was taken to the hospital in New London, and his arm was amputated. He was not expected to survive.

The Germans who came to work at the Rossie mill in Mystic and at American Velvet formed one of the town's largest immigrant groups in the early twentieth century. It was such a large group that German-language classes were taught at Stonington High School for many years.

While factory work was difficult and dangerous, the employees formed close-knit communities, participated in local parades, formed their own recreational teams and were treated to annual picnics by their employers. The Rossie mill sponsored two-day summer picnics featuring two live bands, a temporary beer hall and a portable dance floor.

In Mystic, Germans established the Social Society Frohsinn. Its clubhouse still stands on Greenmanville Avenue across from Mystic Seaport. Pabst Blue Ribbon brewery presented the club with its bar. During Prohibition in the 1920s, the club brewed its own beer.

American Velvet moved to Stonington from the Astoria section of Queens after a malaria outbreak in New York. Stonington's American Velvet workers formed the Arion Singing Society in 1894 and bought their own clubhouse in 1909. In 1940, the building, complete with a kitchen, books, pool tables and two bowling alleys, became the first home of the Stonington Ambulance Corps. Clarence Wimpfheimer, who ran American Velvet at the time, also was a generous community leader at the forefront of the formation of the Stonington Ambulance Corps. He donated a Cadillac ambulance to the group and, in 1946, bought a fire engine for Stonington Borough.

In lower Pawcatuck, another factory lured English workers. Operators of the Clark thread mill also developed a neighborhood of houses and rented them to workers. The streets there were given British names such as Buckingham and Cleveland. Fish-and-chips vendors hawked food throughout the neighborhood, a church was established to provide a place for workers to worship and a local watering hole had the decidedly British moniker Piccadilly Pub. The proliferation of British workers also gave rise to the sport of boxing in Pawcatuck, and weekend soccer matches near the mill routinely attracted more than one thousand spectators.

By the time of the Great Depression of the 1930s, Clark's Village was the last mill-owned residential neighborhood in town, *The Day* of New London reported. Workers' rents were not covering the expense of owning the houses, however. So, in 1937, the mill owners announced that they would auction the village comprising ten duplex houses, ten single-family houses, the church and a small library.

The Depression was just one reason for the gradual decline in manufacturing in Mystic and Stonington. German assets were seized at the

Rossie Velvet Company workers enjoyed annual summer picnics in the early 1900s. *Courtesy Mystic River Historical Society Inc., Mystic, Connecticut.*

The former Rossie Velvet mill in Mystic is now the home of Mystic Seaport Museum's Collections Research Center. *Courtesy Mystic River Historical Society Inc., Mystic, Connecticut.*

Many German immigrants came to Stonington to work at American Velvet in the borough. *Courtesy Stonington Historical Society, American Velvet Collection.*

Rossie mill during World War I, bitter strikes plagued some factories and the Clark mill was severely damaged in the New England hurricane of 1938. Still, in a town tricentennial booklet published in 1949, more than twenty-five industries are listed as operating in town.

"Industrial Stonington today employs nearly 3,000 people and these same people, when combined, receive in one year over $8,000,000.00 in wages. The property value as compiled from a recent questionnaire, exceeds $10,000,000.00," according to the booklet put together by the Industries Committee of the Stonington Tricentennial.

By 2018, much of that once thriving industrial base was gone. Some former mills have been converted for other uses. One half of the former Clark mill, which is owned by two separate entities, has been redeveloped as apartments. Mills in Mystic and Old Mystic have long served as office buildings. The former American Velvet mill houses a variety of small businesses and a winter farmers' market. The former Rossie mill houses Mystic Seaport's archives.

While the looms and sewing machines ceased operating, many descendants of the immigrants who left their European homelands to head to Stonington and Mystic a century or more ago still live in town. Some of the institutions they built—Mystic's German club, Pawcatuck's Italo-American Club and the borough's Portuguese Holy Ghost Society among them—continue to help keep the distinct European cultures of the long-ago immigrants alive.

5
WOMEN OF DISTINCTION

In 1654, the land that later would become the town of Stonington was heavily wooded and sparsely settled. Captain George Denison brought his second wife, Lady Ann Borodell Denison, to establish a home in that expanse.

While Captain Denison was a man of position among European settlers, he could not immediately offer Lady Ann a life of material luxury in still comparatively primitive colonial Connecticut. A member of a fairly wealthy and noble family in Ireland, she gave up a more comfortable lifestyle in Europe to join her husband in the outpost. In Stonington, she had few close neighbors and little female camaraderie. Her house and its amenities were cruder than where she had lived in Europe, and her husband was often away from home. In addition, she was caring for six young children.

Lady Ann is one of many courageous women who have called Stonington and Mystic home. Some were from relatively powerful and wealthy families. Some were well known in their time but have slipped from the public's memory. Many others lived and died in obscurity but also contributed to the fabric of the region.

While Lady Ann Denison is one of the earlier examples of Stonington's prominent women, there were countless others. Contemporary examples include Ruth Buzzi, whose childhood home was in the Wequetequock section of town. The comedian was well known to fans of the 1960s television show *Rowan & Martin's Laugh-In*. Her character Gladys Ormphby became a household name from coast to coast.

There were others as well. Margaret and Mary Dreier, two progressive sisters active in the woman suffrage movement and many social justice issues at the turn of the twentieth century, built a summer home called Shawondasee in Stonington in 1904. Elise Owen, who was born in New London in 1898, lived in Linden Hall in Stonington and was one of the few licensed female commercial pilots in the early years of aviation. She gave flying instruction at the former Wequetequock airport, where Saltwater Farm Vineyard is currently located. She was sometimes visited locally by her friend Amelia Earhart.

In addition to these notable women, the Fort Rachel neighborhood of Mystic was named for an actual woman named Rachel who lived beneath the great rock outcropping in the area and was said to be garrulous and to have the gift of second sight, a phenomenon later known as extrasensory perception.

There also were the many teachers who guided, educated and disciplined generations of Stonington schoolchildren. Teaching was long one of the few professions open to women, and the public expected teachers to be more than educators. Before central heating, they built the fires needed to keep schoolrooms warm. They also helped young children put on and take off coats, boots and other outer garments and sometimes provided clean clothing for less fortunate children. They played the roles of mother, counselor, confidante, sister and disciplinarian. Many students remembered their teachers most for this latter role. It wasn't unusual for teachers in the nineteenth and early twentieth centuries to be very strict. A former student had what was a typical memory of an Old Mystic teacher: a stern spinster who kept a rubber hose handy to inflict punishment.

SACRIFICING CONVENTION FOR LOVE

Mary Burtch of Stonington was eighteen years old when she married William Brewster on March 23, 1841. The couple enjoyed just three months together before William left on a whaling voyage to New Zealand as master of the ship *Philetus*. Mary waited at home, as was typical of whaling wives in the mid-nineteenth century.

By the couple's fourth wedding anniversary, they had spent just five months together. Mary Brewster decided that a life of waiting in port for her husband's return was not for her. So, when Captain William Brewster sailed out of Stonington on the whaleship *Tiger* on November 4, 1845, Mary left with him. It was an unusual decision.

Whaling voyages were far from attractive for anyone. While lucrative for a few, whaling was a dangerous occupation that required months, even years, of isolation on the seas, combined with short, adrenaline-inducing and harrowing periods chasing whales. After the catch, the dirty work of processing the carcasses aboard ship followed. *She Was a Sister Sailor*, a book compiling Mary Brewster's whaling journals published in 1992 by the Mystic Seaport and edited by Joan Druett, recounts that Stonington residents viewed whaling as risky and expensive. Crew members often were secured only through trickery and coercion.

For women, taking an extended voyage was uncommon, although not unique. Although not on whalers, at least three Stonington wives went to sea with their husbands before Brewster's decision, and accounts of women at sea are still being discovered. Brewster may have been inspired by those she knew had already dared to sail. She likely inspired others to join their husbands at sea. At a time when women were taught to be demure and patient, there was much societal pressure against such an undertaking. After she announced her decision, Brewster was disowned by her stepmother, who had raised her from the time she was a child.

But Brewster loved her husband deeply, and no public shame or familial threat would dissuade her. In another book, *Petticoat Whaler*, Druett records some of the words from Mary's journals: "She who has extended a mother's love and watchfulness over me said her consent would never be given. In no way would she assist me and if I left her she thought me very ungrateful and lastly though not least Her home would never be a home for me again." Mary seemed unconcerned, however. "Well, thank Heaven it is all past and I am on board of the good ship Tiger with my dear Husband," she wrote.

Although Brewster didn't regret her decision, life aboard the ship would not prove easy. Her quarters were cramped. She was not allowed on the forward part of the deck, because it was considered too rough a place for women. She suffered long bouts of seasickness, especially when the wind was light but the seas rough. She was away from Stonington for nearly a year before she met another woman.

Druett writes that Brewster met Sarah Frisbie Gray, wife of Captain Slumon Gray, of another Stonington ship, the *Newburyport*, in Lahaina, Maui, Hawaii. Brewster noted in her journal that she was very happy to see a "sister sailor." Gray first sailed in 1844.

Mary Brewster joined her husband, Captain William Brewster, aboard the whaleship *Tiger* out of Stonington in the mid-1800s. *From the collection of the Stonington Historical Society.*

The *Tiger* left Maui for the coast of California then returned to what were then known as the Sandwich Islands in March 1847. Brewster's husband made her stay on shore in Maui for a six-month period while the ship again went to sea, headed for whaling grounds. She was angry and sad to be left behind, although she did have the company of other captains' wives while on the island. When the *Tiger* again fetched her, she discovered that her movement aboard would be even more restricted. The space that had been her sewing cabin was now being used by the mates.

Brewster's journal entries give a glimpse of her life at sea, time that seems punctuated by long hours of tedium combined with periods of taxing labor. Karlee Turner, a Mystic Seaport role player, shares many of those entries on her blog *America's Victorian Era in the Age of Sail: Women at Sea*. On July 2, 1846, Brewster wrote, "Blowing hard and rainy weather. All hands busy in stowing down and clearing up decks which were very full this morning. I have written two letters and knit the remainder of the day." The following day, she wrote: "One whale sighted, boats have not lowered it being to [*sic*] rough. My employment has been of various kinds, cooking, making poultices for some hands, and numerous small jobs. No chance for idleness here nor lonesome feelings, plenty noise and work."

On Sunday, July 26, 1846, Brewster writes about reading the Bible and seeking to keep the Sabbath in a serene manner. Her peace was disturbed when the crew brought in another whale, boosting the ship's whale oil total to more than one thousand barrels. "During the day I have read several chapters in the bible," she wrote. "And have endeavored to call my thoughts from the business of the day and have them placed more on my own feelings and give some time to reflection." About the whale hunt on the same day, she writes: "At 7 PM boats got fast to a whale, at 9 got him to the ship. Men all singing and bawling doughnuts, doughnuts tomorrow, as this will certainly make us 1,000 bbls and it is custom among the whalemen a bache [sic] of doughnuts to every thousand."

Brewster returned to Stonington in April 1848, about two and a half years after setting sail. Despite its dangers and isolation, or perhaps because she was not readily accepted back into female society in Stonington, she soon again chose life at sea with her husband, leaving with him on a second voyage just fourteen weeks after returning home.

EXPLORING THE GREAT OUTDOORS

On a rural hilltop overlooking River Road and the Mystic River, Mary Jobe strode onto a neighbor's farm one day in the early 1900s with a grand proposition. She asked the farmer to set aside all his produce to supply the nearby camp for girls she planned to open. Locals were not used to encountering such forceful, outspoken women, and the farmer was taken aback.

"She was a stunner," Warren B. Fish recalled in 1987, when telling the tale to local historian Carol Kimball. Fish's father didn't agree to Jobe's demands, but he did sell milk to the camp when it opened in the summer of 1916.

Mary Jobe, later Mary Jobe Akeley, truly was a stunner in all of the ways that word can be understood. Strong and independent, she trekked into the British Columbia wilderness when she was a single woman as early as 1905. She photographed and mapped the region and chronicled the wildlife and the natives who lived there. In 1914, on commission from the Canadian government, she mapped the headwaters of the Fraser River some five hundred miles northeast of Vancouver. She was a teacher, photographer and explorer decades before most women dared to even dream of undertaking such risks. She established her girls' camp near the Mystic River four years before women won the right to vote in the United States, at a time when the idea of promoting vigorous outdoor activity for girls that included archery, hiking, swimming and diving was just starting to become popular in the United States.

She remained single well into her forties. She then married the explorer, naturalist, inventor and taxidermist Carl Akeley, who was twelve years her senior. They married in 1924; the union lasted just two years before he died.

She traveled extensively as a lecturer after she was widowed and wrote numerous books. Despite living most of her life as a single woman, she often was described in terms of her husband's explorations. This is simply how it was for women of her time.

Her *New York Times* obituary on July 22, 1966, noted that she finished her husband's work in Africa when he died while on an expedition in what was then the Belgian Congo. The article went on to report that she was "described by her friends as a 'plucky young brunette'" when she made many trips to uncharted areas of the Canadian Rockies in the early 1900s.

Jobe likely understood the trail she was blazing for women. She once predicted there would come a day when female explorers would be so common that journalists would not seek them out for interviews. Never particularly loved by her Mystic neighbors because of eccentricities that became more pronounced with age, she was nevertheless respected. Locals did, however, call her "the hermit on the hill" in the years just prior to her death at age eighty-eight.

Jobe grew up a farm girl in Tappan, Ohio, about seventy-five miles west of Pittsburgh. She had ancestors who served in the American Revolution, War of 1812 and the Civil War. One ancestor was a director in the East India Company, a powerful trading company chartered by Queen Elizabeth I in 1600.

At a young age, she chose a path that would take her far from small-town farm life. She headed first to undergraduate study at the now defunct Scio College, then to graduate work at Bryn Mawr and, finally, to New York City and Columbia University. By some accounts, she underwent her first expedition into the Canadian wilderness as early as 1905. Other accounts put the year as late as 1911. Either way, she was likely a Bryn Mawr graduate student when she first headed into the wilderness.

She ultimately made several more trips to the region, riding some eight hundred miles on horseback in a single trip and trekking along on one expedition despite suffering from influenza. The Canadian government honored her by naming a mountain for her. She also gained the respect of the far North's native peoples, who came to call her Dene-Sczaki, or "man-woman."

She was a faculty member at New York City's Hunter College when she decided to establish a summer camp for girls. In 1914, she bought forty-five acres of Mystic woodland used for many years to host annual peace activist meetings. The seaside village was a logical choice. It offered the convenience of being on the train line halfway between New York City and Boston. It was remote and peaceful yet accessible to those major urban centers.

Camp Mystic hosted eighty girls annually. An eight-week session cost $375, a sum equal to nearly $9,000 in 2020. Campers came from as far away as Hawaii to spend the summer swimming, learning to dive, practicing archery, listening to lectures by noted explorers, hiking, canoeing, riding horses, doing arts and crafts and staging plays.

In a letter Jobe wrote promoting Camp Mystic, she noted that all of the camp's counselors were college-educated, professional women and that many were teachers. She once explained the camp's mission by saying she believed "girls find health, happiness and their highest development out-of-doors, where they leave behind them the artificialities of towns and cities for the joyous realities of the wooded hills and seashore."

In an undated article in *Good Old Days* magazine, former camper Eliza Know wrote about "Good Old Camp Mystic." In her opinion, the camp uniform of white middy blouses, headbands and bloomers that were "voluminous horrors of navy blue serge" made campers look like a cross between Native American princesses and ballet dancers. Campers slept in tents named for Jobe's Canadian exploration campsites. The tent mates, Know wrote, were "as varied as the contents of an Irish stew."

Know recounted the story of a summer hike in which Jobe, who Know said had the disciplinary characteristics of a Marine Corps drill sergeant, led the girls on a trek ending with an overnight campout near an abandoned Victorian-era hotel on Mystic Island, a place now called Ram Island. Know said that swarms of mosquitoes kept most campers awake; two campers who did manage some sleep awoke to discover they had slumbered on poison ivy. Jobe, however, snored peacefully through the night.

Know also recalled swimming in the Mystic River, which was often fouled by mud and mill waste. Still, the camp offered some luxuries not standard for many American families of the era. It featured, for example, a piano for entertainment, and it had electricity, flush toilets, hot showers and bathtubs.

The camp operated until the financial hardships of the 1929 stock market crash and the resulting Great Depression forced its closure in 1930. Jobe owned the Mystic property for the rest of her life, however, spending many weekends and summers there before moving there more permanently after retiring.

While it was the camp that brought her to southeastern Connecticut, its operation always was a sideline. Most of her time was spent teaching in New York City. In 1920, Mary Jobe met Carl Akeley, a noted natural scientist who worked for several museums, including the American Museum of Natural History in the city. The couple married four years later, and she gave up her career at his request, instead supporting Akeley's ventures. In 1926, the couple set out on an eight-month journey through Africa, exploring Kenya, Uganda and what was then the Belgian Congo. Carl Akeley was collecting specimens, taking photographs and studying wildlife. The information was used in planning the New York City museum's Africa Hall. Akeley was a veteran to such arduous expeditions and believed to be almost indestructible. His health failed him on this particularly rigorous journey, however. He died and was buried in what was then termed "gorilla country" in the Congo.

Instead of heading home, his wife completed the expedition. She returned to visit her husband's remote grave site twenty years after his death. By 1979, many years after her visit, the grave had been decimated by local poachers.

The Museum of Natural History named its Africa Hall in honor of the couple. "Mary L. Jobe Akeley belongs to that band of fearless women who have not merely accompanied their men to the remote danger spots of the globe, but have carried on the work of their male companions when illness, accident, even death, have felled them," museum staff wrote on a flier promoting one of her lectures there.

Mary Jobe Akeley spent much of the rest of her life writing magazine articles for the likes of *Harper's* and the *Canadian Alpine Journal* and books focused on African wildlife. She also advocated for land and wildlife conservation, lectured extensively and received several honors. Among these is one of Belgium's highest honors: the Cross of the Knight, Order of the Crown, which she was awarded in 1928. She was the only woman at the inaugural ceremonies in Brussels for Parc National Albert. Established in 1925 primarily to protect endangered mountain gorillas, it was the first national park in Africa. Now called Virunga National Park, it has unfortunately been extensively damaged due to political conflict in the region. It was closed to the public in 2018.

Jobe Akeley also later was named to both the Connecticut and Ohio women's halls of fame.

Left: Carl and Mary Jobe Akeley were explorers and naturalists who married in 1924. *Courtesy of the Akeley Trust, care of Mystic River Historical Society Inc., Mystic, Connecticut.*

Right: Mary Jobe ran Camp Mystic for girls from 1916 until the Great Depression forced its closure in 1930. *Courtesy Mystic River Historical Society Inc., Mystic, Connecticut.*

In 1937, in reflecting on her life in Connecticut, she wrote: "In my home in the oak and cedar forest of Great Hill, Mystic, Connecticut, I found for many years a happy environment in which to carry forward my project of out-of-door education of young people....I now find in this same spot, the peace and refreshment in a quiet and beautiful environment necessary for creative work. At the end of my busy days there, I enjoy a mental and physical relaxation in the unspoiled countryside."

In her later years, she grew more eccentric and likely suffered from dementia. She was at best a pack rat and at worst a hoarder whose house became cluttered and unkempt. Nonetheless, it was also the repository of a treasure-trove of trinkets and mementos from the exotic places she traveled to. She remained independent, direct and forthright to the end. She traveled by herself to Mexico when she was in her eighties. Long after her death, *The*

Campers came from near and far to hike, swim and learn about nature at Camp Mystic. *Courtesy Mystic River Historical Society Inc., Mystic, Connecticut.*

Compass newspaper of Mystic published an article about her. In it, a Mystic ambulance driver recalled the day Mary Jobe Akeley called for emergency medical transport. She told the driver that she was ill and needed to go to a hospital in Boston. The ambulance headed toward the city with her on board, but on the way, she decided she was feeling more fit. She told the driver to keep going, however. Instead of the hospital, she asked to be dropped off at a favorite Boston hotel.

In the final years of her life, she arranged to donate her Mystic land to preserve it in perpetuity. She died in 1966 at Mystic's Mary Elizabeth Nursing Center. Her beloved Mystic property on the so-called Great Hill is now a nature preserve managed by the Denison Pequotsepos Nature Center. It is aptly called the Peace Sanctuary. Each spring, some four hundred rare wild pink lady's slippers bloom there.

KEEPING NATIVE CULTURE

In the 1950s, when popular culture was steeped in the image of Indians as bad guys war-whooping across movie screens and most Connecticut residents thought Native Americans had long ago disappeared from the state, Eva Lutz Butler testified at a legislative hearing in Hartford on behalf of the Pequot tribe. A local sportsmen's club was trying to acquire some of the land deeded to the Pequots after the powerful tribe was defeated by colonial troops in the 1600s.

Butler, a historian, anthropologist and archaeologist who tirelessly researched and chronicled Native American history, stood up on behalf of the few mostly impoverished and powerless tribal members still living on the Ledyard reservation. It would be many decades, and long after Butler's death, before a rejuvenated Pequot tribe won federal recognition and the right to develop part of that same tribal land known as Mashantucket into Foxwoods Resort Casino, the world's third-largest casino in a 2018 rating. Those who knew Butler best said she would have been delighted by the tribe's contemporary position as an economic powerhouse with international stature.

Butler lived for decades in Ledyard. She is best known locally for the small but important Old Mystic local history center she helped found. The Indian and Colonial Research Center is a repository of information on local tribes, genealogy, historic buildings and other local history, much of it the result of Butler's own research. Housed in an 1856 brick building that was once the Mystic Bank, the center includes reminders of the past, books, papers, photographs and artifacts. Fittingly, it was from these archives that the Mashantucket Pequots were able to find much of the information they needed to gain federal recognition in 1983.

Born in Pleasantville, New Jersey, Butler moved to southeastern Connecticut in 1928 when her husband, S.B. Butler, was appointed as the first superintendent of Groton schools. At the time, the state was revving up for its 1935 tercentenary celebration, and Butler eagerly jumped into the local preparations. She researched and developed a map of pre-1800 homes and homesites in Groton, and she helped establish the Fort Hill Indian Memorial Association, which erected a replica of an early settler's home at the top of Groton's Fort Hill. The hill, located near Fitch High School, was the site of a 1637 Pequot fort. The replica home operated for a time as a museum of Indian and colonial artifacts.

Butler became fascinated with Native American history after her son found an arrowhead in New York City's Central Park, she once told a friend. That small discovery launched a lifetime of study, research, teaching and collecting. She earned a bachelor's degree from the University of New Mexico in 1941 and a master's of science degree from the University of Pennsylvania in 1946.

In Connecticut, she became well acquainted with both the Mohegan and Pequot tribes and was involved in some of the earliest archaeological excavations at Fort Shantok in Montville, a site historically and culturally important to the Mohegan tribe. Beginning in 1947 and extending until two years before her death in 1969, she taught popular extension courses on local history, archaeology, nature study, colonial literature and local lore for Eastern Connecticut State University. The classes were conducted in the family's colonial-era house in Ledyard and sometimes featured open-hearth cooking lessons.

While she did not drive, she never had difficulty finding a friend willing to chauffeur her to town halls or libraries, where she spent hours conducting research and taking copious notes. One of Butler's close friends, Mystic historian Carol Kimball, told the *New York Times* in 1983 that at the time of Butler's death she had amassed some thirty-five hundred books and more than two thousand loose-leaf notebooks, along with Indian artifacts, a collection of eighteenth- and nineteenth-century school primers and many boxes of old photographs. Butler's 1969 *New York Times* obituary reported that the collection was kept in six of her home's fourteen rooms.

Eva Butler was an anthropologist, historian and archaeologist who studied Native American history and culture. She was instrumental in establishing Old Mystic's Indian & Colonial Research Center. *Courtesy Indian & Colonial Research Center Incorporated, Old Mystic, Connecticut.*

The village of Old Mystic. The bank building that is now the home of the Indian & Colonial Research Center is at left. *Courtesy Indian & Colonial Research Center Inc., Old Mystic, Connecticut.*

The impetus to establish the Indian and Colonial Research Center came after Butler was hospitalized for a month following a 1965 heart attack. She then became concerned about what would become of her extensive, largely unpublished, uncatalogued and unorganized research. She and a group of friends and acquaintances then bought the vacant historic bank building for one dollar from the Town of Stonington, secured a $2,000 grant from the Bodenwein Public Benevolent Foundation in New London and established the Indian and Colonial Research Center. While her collection formed the core of the center's archives, Butler was adamant that the center should not be named for her.

In addition to the Indian and Colonial Research Center, Butler was also a founder of Exeter, Rhode Island's Tomaquag Museum focusing on the history of the Narragansett tribe. She also was instrumental in establishing the Thames Science Center in New London, now relocated in Newport, Rhode Island. But the heart of her lifelong work in anthropology, history and genealogy remains housed in the tiny Old Mystic Indian and Colonial Research Center, where, years after Butler's death, volunteers continue to work organizing and cataloguing her research. The center remains a vital resource. If not for Eva Butler, much of the knowledge at the center might otherwise have been lost.

6

Only in Mystic and Stonington

Every community has its unique characters who become local icons. Stonington and Mystic are no exception. One such person was Zebulon Hancox, an eccentric man who lived in the borough in the nineteenth century. Legend has it that the love of his life spurned him due to his poverty, so he set out to amass as much money as possible. He did this, in part, by making everything he used, including all his own clothing and even his own wood buttons. Some of his artifacts are now on display at Stonington's Old Lighthouse Museum.

Hancox is hardly the only character who had local connections. Here are the stories of some others.

An Eternal Dispute

At the corner of North Main and Palmer Streets, surrounded by a tall stone wall and isolated from the final resting places of other citizens, sits one of Stonington's most unusual and curious graves. The grave is that of John W. Richmond and his wife, Henrietta, who were not residents of Stonington for the preponderance of their lives and had little to do with the town. Instead, John Richmond, a Providence, Rhode Island physician who died in 1857, chose to be buried in Stonington because of the town's location just outside the boundary of his home state.

The Medical World: A Journal of Universal Medical Intelligence, published in Boston by Damrell & Moore and George Coolidge in 1857, reports Dr. Richmond's death in Philadelphia. Of the unusual terms of his burial, the journal reports:

> *His remains were brought to Stonington and deposited in a tomb on Saturday. Dr. Richmond was eminent in his profession, and businesslike in all his undertakings. He has long been at war with the State of Rhode Island, on account of her repudiation of her Revolutionary debt, and carried his antipathy so far that he purchased a burial lot in Stonington, Conn. and donated $500 to the town to keep it in repair, that his remains might rest in soil uncontaminated by forgetfulness of the services of the men of the Revolution.*

Richmond also chose to have the outline of this story engraved on the obelisk that marks his grave. Chiseled there, it reads:

> *When Rhode Island, by her legislation from 1844 to 1850, REPUDIATED her REVOLUTIONARY Debt, Dr. Richmond removed from that STATE to this BOROUGH and selected this as his Family Burial Place; unwilling that the remains of himself and his family should be disgraced by being a part of the common earth of a REPUDIATING STATE.*

Many Rhode Island leaders had a much different viewpoint, however. They contended that it was Richmond who was the disgrace.

Just two years before his death, Richmond published three booklets densely packed with details of the cause that led him to be buried outside Rhode Island. Rhode Island, as was the case with other American colonies, financed part of the high cost of fighting the American Revolution by issuing debt certificates. In essence, patriotic citizens eager to find ways to support the cause for independence bought the notes. They were promised to be repaid in full plus interest. An estimated 14 percent of the cost of the Revolution was paid for in this manner, according to a February 23, 2015 article, "How Was the Revolutionary War Paid For?" by John L. Smith Jr. in the *Journal of the American Revolution*. The problem for those who bought these debt certificates, however, is that they were not always repaid in full, plus interest, as promised. In addition, colonies that became states after independence also owed soldiers and sailors who fought the war, and sometimes their heirs, for their services.

The states struggled to repay these debts. As an example, Richmond details the case of Mary Rhodes, who died at age ninety-eight in 1852.

"She was the last surviving creditor holding a certificate in her own name," Richmond wrote. "This was issued in renewal of a portion of her claim for $462.53, presented and allowed under the act of 1795. She was then paid $385.44 and a balance certificate given her for $77.09. In 1844, she petitioned over her own signature for the payment of her balance certificate, and her petition was laid on the table, members of the House denying the debt as due from the State.

"This claim originated in the services of her late husband, Sylvester Rhodes, of Warwick, he having died in 1780 with disease contracted on board the Jersey Prison Ship, where he was held a prisoner. This claim is no solitary case," Richmond wrote. "In many cases the holders are suffering all the evils and privations attendant on very limited means of support."

Because Richmond was born in 1775 and so was just an infant during the Revolution, he had no personal experience in the war. Perhaps he simply was repulsed by the notion that those who were the most patriotic and loyal to the cause were also those left with empty promises and no money. Perhaps in his practice as a physician he too often encountered destitute patients who should have been enjoying financial stability if the state had not reneged on its debts.

Dr. John W. Richmond was a nineteenth-century Rhode Island physician who insisted on being buried in Stonington because of a dispute with his home state. *Photo taken by the author.*

Or, perhaps, he was seeking to repair his reputation. While his cause at first drew admiration in his lifetime, he later was ridiculed and belittled as a fraud. Many Rhode Island officials said Richmond took advantage of his position as a respected physician and businessman to make obscure and unsubstantiated financial claims.

Wilkins Updike, a member of Rhode Island's general assembly, wrote, "I have been long convinced that the obscurity of the origin of these claims has been the only reason that they have gained any credit at all."

While Richmond presented himself as a martyr, others contended that he was little more than a thief. "At length an impression became general that a game was being played, not in the interest of soldiers and their descendants, but of a gang of unprincipled and unscrupulous speculators," notes an article in an April 1896 Rhode Island Historical Society publication.

Despite the likelihood that Richmond's cause célèbre was not what he claimed, his decision to be buried in Connecticut and have his reasons chiseled in the stone of his grave ensure that his cause, no matter what launched it, lives on.

Engineering and Art

"Well dearest mother, it certainly is time you should hear from your truant son, who has been away now for more than a month!" So begins an October 10, 1855 letter written by James McNeill Whistler to his mother after a transatlantic trip brought him to London to pursue his dream of making a living as an artist. Whistler would not return to the United States, but many in the small seaside town of Stonington where the family lived for a time would long remember the difficult curly haired child and be patrons of his work.

"Love to all in Stonington," Whistler signed off the 1855 letter that is now part of a collection of some seven thousand pieces of Whistler correspondence held by the University of Glasgow in Scotland. Whistler's mother was of Scottish descent, and the collection was donated to the university by Whistler's sister-in-law, who inherited his estate.

Stonington came to know the Whistler family in the 1830s, when George Washington Whistler moved his family there. The elder Whistler was one of the foremost civil engineers of the era, and his work for the Providence and Stonington Railroad helped transform the village to a bustling industrial and transportation hub.

George Washington Whistler was born in Indiana, attended West Point and, after graduating, moved frequently throughout the upper Midwest and Northeast as he worked on a variety of projects. He was an assistant professor of drawing at West Point, helped plot the international boundary at Lake Superior and worked for the Baltimore & Ohio Railroad and on the locks at Lowell, Massachusetts.

His first wife died very young, leaving him a widower with three young children. He then married the sister of a close friend. George Whistler and

Anna Mathilda McNeill had five sons, including the future artist James McNeill Whistler, whom Anna dubbed Jemie.

James Whistler was born in Lowell in 1834 and moved with his family to Stonington when he was about three years old. His mother's sister lived in the village with her husband, who was a member of the long-established Stonington family the Palmers. The Whistlers settled near the Palmers in a house on Main Street as George Whistler worked to develop the Providence and Stonington Railroad.

The importance of the elder Whistler's work cannot be overstated. In an August 1949 article in *Connecticut Circle* magazine, author H.F. Thomas called George Whistler the "father of practical railroads."

Before the line linking southeastern Connecticut to Providence opened in 1837, those traveling between New York City and Boston were forced to take a much longer water route to Rhode Island's capital city. After the railroad was completed between Providence and Stonington, the trip became less arduous.

Thomas points out that it was Whistler who made some design changes, such as including cabs for locomotives. These changes aimed directly at increasing railroad employee health and comfort. "A large measure of the successful operation of both the Stonington and western railroads may be ascribed to the fidelity of the employees," Thomas writes in the magazine article.

Besides George Whistler's contributions to the success of the Stonington railroad line, residents remembered the Whistlers for other reasons. A chapter on the Whistlers in the 1913 book *Stonington by the Sea* points out that George Whistler retrofitted a carriage with wheels designed to run on the railroad tracks to enable a quicker trip to Westerly, Rhode Island, each Sunday, where the family attended services at the Episcopal church.

Of James, they recalled the child as small and witty. He loved to pull pranks and sat sketching for hours. He also could be difficult. Rieta B. Palmer, who wrote the chapter, reported, "It was said that no one could live in harmony with him for long."

The family lived in Stonington only until 1840, when another railroad engineering job took George Whistler to Springfield, Massachusetts. In 1842, his engineering services were sought by Czar Nicholas I of Russia, who was seeking to build a railroad linking St. Petersburg and Moscow. After George left for Russia, Anna and the children returned to Stonington for a time but then joined George Whistler overseas. James began his formal art study in Russia but returned to Connecticut after George died from cholera in St. Petersburg in 1849.

James Whistler tried to follow in his father's footsteps, entering the military academy at West Point. His poor grades and bad attitude toward authority led to his dismissal after three years, however. His mother's hopes that he'd become a minister also were dashed.

Whistler instead was determined to become an artist. In 1855, he headed to Europe to make his dream a reality. His reputation in the art world rose through the late 1800s, although his viewpoints, compositions and subjects were sometimes controversial and his finances not always stable. In 1871, Whistler produced what would become his most famous painting, although it barely escaped rejection by London's Royal Academy. The painting, titled *Arrangement in Grey and Black No. 1*, is more commonly known as *Whistler's Mother*. The portrait of Anna McNeill Whistler, seated in profile, is notable for its severe and sparse composition and dark, almost monochrome palette.

In April 1872, Anna Whistler wrote a letter mentioning two of her sons' precarious financial conditions and their need to help care for her. She, like many women of her day, struggled financially after her husband's death. "Their struggles are so unwearied to attain position to enable them to keep bright their gain & gain an honest livelihood.

The Whistler family, including artist James McNeill Whistler, lived in this house in Stonington Borough for a time in the 1800s. *Collotype Company postcard, courtesy Mystic Seaport Museum.*

Both their professions involve unavoidable expense, with the strictest self denial & practical economy—as yet the income so inadequate to cover expences [*sic*]. But I know all the discipline must be safest & best for them. I am always sorry to be an additional care," she wrote.

While her famous son demonstrated no desire to return to his childhood home in Stonington, residents there did not forget him.

Anna Whistler, on the other hand, always loved Stonington. Her sister lived there, and her husband so desired to return to the village that he is buried there. He remains one of the most notable residents of Stonington Cemetery.

A MYSTIC SHOWMAN

More than a decade before Mystic Seaport was established in 1929, another well-known Mystic museum drew visitors. In 1917, Charles Q. Eldredge opened a private museum near his Old Mystic home. It was stocked with a wide assortment of souvenirs and curios—some genuine and some fake—from around the world. The museum attracted hundreds, possibly thousands, of visitors annually.

"Riverview, this one-man museum, is Mr. Eldredge's boyhood home, remodeled and enlarged," a *Hartford Courant* reporter wrote in an article published in December 1926. Eldredge claimed some two thousand visitors annually and more than seven thousand items in his collection. "Flags and windmills, guns and birdhouses, first attract the visitor's eye and then he is stopped by astonishment at the sight of a mounted skeleton of a tremendous right whale whose jaw bones alone measure 18 feet. The next thing he knows, Mr. Eldredge is saying, 'come right in,' and then he is looking at marvels he has not dreamt of and hearing wondrous tales."

Eldredge spent his boyhood in Old Mystic and reportedly always had a bit of P.T. Barnum–style hucksterism in him. He untruthfully announced to an especially strict teacher one day that his middle initial was "Q." His classmates thought this hilarious. Eldredge later legally incorporated the *Q* into his name.

In his autobiography, Eldredge said his brain was impacted when he fell off an oxcart as a child, hitting his head on a stone. Whether because of this fall or simply because of his personal biology, Eldredge was a quirky, eccentric character.

Helen May Clarke, whose girlhood journals were published as the book *An Account of My Life*, commented about her visit to Eldredge's museum in 1922. "We drove up to Charles Q's museum. He is a relation of some sort—don't think the Eldredge line comes in except by marriage," wrote the Mystic girl. "He made fortunes and lost them and made them again. He built the mansion on the River, bought yachts and fine horses. He has been married twice or more and his son shot himself in a hunting lodge on Lovers Leap, on account of a chorus girl."

Eldredge was born in 1845, the youngest of eight children. While he enjoyed his Mystic boyhood, he left the village as a teenager. He settled in Hoosick Falls, New York, located northeast of Troy and near the southern Vermont border. There, he made a comfortable living in the lumber business. He also traveled around the globe, collecting the souvenirs and curios that would make up a portion of his museum collection.

When in his mid-forties, he returned to Old Mystic, where he attracted much local attention both for the museum he built and stocked with global treasures and trinkets, as well as for his other eccentricities. For example, he built a Mississippi River–style stern-wheel steamboat that he ran on the Mystic River. The riverboat greeted with a hearty toot of its horn the first trolley to run into Old Mystic village, according to a column written by local historian Carol Sommer and published in *The Day* of New London in May 2018.

"He built himself boats and models, he built toys and furniture, he wrote the autobiography and he arranged and catalogued the collection of curios and now he is the busy, happy curator of the museum he has himself founded," the *Courant* reported in 1926. "Mr. Eldredge is like a boy who has fifty new persons to show his stamp collection to every day in the year and whose interest in the collection has a magic growth from every exhibition."

Included in the collection, the *Courant* reported, were items ranging from a walrus-tusk necklace and ship models to a handcrafted tablecloth from a South Sea island and rare coins. In a curio guidebook he published in 1926, Eldredge describes a few of his treasures. Among them are a cucumber preserved in copper paint, a photograph of a ninety-three-year-old woman on horseback and a glass eye from a swordfish. Eldredge also claimed that a piece of rope in the collection was used to hang a murderer during the Civil War and that an egg cup at the museum belonged to cannibals.

While cabinets of curiosities were found in many sailors' homes, Eldredge's collection attracted plenty of visitors because of the vast quantity of items, as well as the huge variety. This was an era when world travel was reserved

Charles Q. Eldredge ran a popular museum of curiosities in Old Mystic between 1917 and 1937. *Courtesy Mystic River Historical Society Inc., Mystic, Connecticut.*

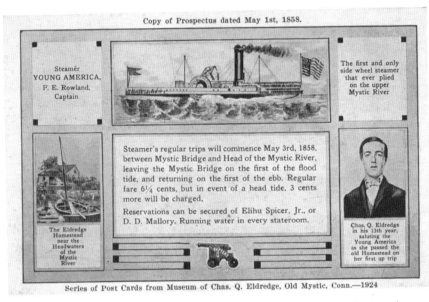

Besides operating a popular museum, Charles Q. Eldredge also ran a steamboat on the Mystic River. *Courtesy Mystic River Historical Society Inc., Mystic, Connecticut.*

for the wealthiest and no television or computers were available to bring the globe's treasures to the average person's consciousness. In addition, Eldredge himself was a source of fascination. He was every bit the showman, although his manner didn't endear him to all.

"Grandmother doesn't approve of him," Clarke wrote in her journal. "He really is an extraordinary person. I should be up there half the time but for one thing. It's like this—as a relative and a friend of Capt. Rhodes—[Clarke's great-grandfather]—it seems perfectly proper for him to act affectionate, but he isn't affectionate in a proper way, he likes to pet me. He isn't in his second childhood although ninety I guess, [he was actually in his 70s at this point] and his mind is as sharp as a knife, but well, he is like that. Mother says he always acted silly over women and there's no fool like an old fool."

Eldredge was ninety-two when he died in 1937. His collection was sold at auction. Mystic's version of Barnum's greatest show on earth was scattered as visitors' attentions were now drawn to the historic, and authentic, Mystic Seaport Museum.

7

EVENTS FORGE COMMUNITY

In 1773, two doctors opened a hospital on an island near Stonington to provide inoculations against smallpox. While fighting a disease that killed one in six who contracted it might seem a noble cause, local residents at the time feared the hospital's presence would cause the disease to spread. Violent objections forced the hospital's closure.

This local event is one among many that have shaped the community. Some events were momentous: the August 1814 Battle of Stonington in which locals rebuffed a British attack, for example. Another event that had national consequence was the 1880 collision of the steamships *Narragansett* and *Stonington*. One survivor of that disaster decided he'd been spared in order to carry out a momentous act. That act was the assassination of President James Garfield.

Other events are not as familiar but nonetheless played pivotal roles in shaping the community.

PEACE LOVERS IN MYSTIC

On August 23, 1883, the *New York Times*, under a headline reading "The Mystic Peace Meeting—An Indian Princess from Boston Entertains the Audience," a reporter began his coverage of the annual event in this manner: "Around 12 cocoanuts, 2 bunches of bananas, an industrious man with an accordian and an 'Indian Princess' from Boston. 1,000 persons clustered today in the Mystic woods. The big peace meeting of Connecticut was underway."

While this *Times* reporter was obviously less than impressed by the peace meeting and its messages, going on to poke fun at the lack of clams in Mystic clam chowder and calling into question the authenticity of the Indian princess, thousands of others—indeed, even tens of thousands—were drawn to and fervently believed in the messages of the annual peace meetings that took place on Mystic's Great Hill off River Road for some forty years following the Civil War.

Just two years after this article appeared, for example, the *Hartford Courant* reported that an estimated ten thousand people were attending the conference. The August conferences regularly drew nationally known speakers such as William Lloyd Garrison, Belva Lockwood and Julia Ward Howe.

The peace conferences overseen by the Universal Peace Union took stands far ahead of their times: advocating woman suffrage as early as 1870, denouncing Ku Klux Klan violence in 1871 and annually calling for an end to war that most people today equate with the anti–Vietnam War protests of the 1960s. In 1901, a speaker from Philadelphia told the conference that the greatest obstacle blocking peace was oppression of African American citizens and Jim Crow laws.

The Mystic peace meetings were the 1967 "Summer of Love," the 1960s civil rights movement, the 1910s suffragette movement and the Vietnam-era antiwar protests all rolled into one and repeated annually. The peace conferences were a counterreaction to the deep divisions, carnage and destruction of the Civil War. About 620,000 men lost their lives fighting in the war, a number that represents about 2 percent of the population at the time, according to information from the National Battlefield Trust. More than 6 million would die today if 2 percent of the U.S. population were killed.

Further, the trust points out that many more Civil War casualties resulted from disease and primitive medical treatments. For every three who died on the battlefield, another five died of disease. A quarter of those who left for the war never returned. Many who did return were missing limbs or were physically or emotionally disabled to the point they could no longer work. Physical limitations were especially debilitating given that most contemporary jobs demanded tough physical labor.

About 1,200 Connecticut men were killed in action and another nearly 4,000 died from their wounds or disease. The state's total population in 1860 was about 460,000. In the years following the war, more than 135 memorials and monuments were erected in towns throughout the state, including one that still stands in downtown Mystic.

The war's consequences spurred the peace movement, and many of its most ardent supporters also had been active abolitionists before the war. The Connecticut Peace Society, an outgrowth of the Universal Peace Union established in 1866, formed in 1867. The state group drew membership largely from the ranks of the Rogerene Quakers of Ledyard. Just one year later and three years after the end of the Civil War, the first summer peace meeting was held in a grove near the west bank of the Mystic River at a spot still known as the Peace Sanctuary.

The most radical members of the peace movement rejected any manner of violence, even in the case of self-defense. The appropriately named Alfred H. Love, the Philadelphia Quaker who was the Union's president, even spoke scornfully of those who had fought in the Civil War, heedless of the relatively fresh graves of Mystic veterans buried at Elm Grove Cemetery, which could be seen from the peace grove. When Love was chastised for his views by an angry local, Love agreed that the soldiers had patriotic motives, but he steadfastly refused to sanction any violence, especially that which played out on the battlefield.

Another nationally known figure who frequented the peace conferences was Belva Lockwood. She was a women's rights activist who ran for president in both 1884 and 1888 as a candidate of the National Equal Rights party. Although her candidacy occurred long before U.S. women were granted the vote in 1920, she believed that running for president was an important symbolic effort.

Many men of the era ridiculed and lampooned Lockwood. Newspaper editors warned against the dangers of rule by women. In many communities, local men dressed as women and paraded through the streets in an act of political satire. In October 1884, the *Stonington Mirror* reported that some two hundred men, some carrying dolls, brooms and lighted torches, paraded through the Mystic streets as part of a Belva Lockwood Mother Hubbard Parade aimed at both protesting against and poking fun of Lockwood's candidacy. In 1888, Stonington Borough was the site of a similar parade, this one attracting a crowd of five hundred.

While male powerbrokers of the time didn't approve of Lockwood and others who flocked to the peace conference, many in Mystic eagerly got into the spirit of the conference. The conferences carried serious messages but also were characterized by a lighthearted, party-like atmosphere. Mystic businesspeople and entrepreneurs were only too happy to cash in on the event, with industrious wagon owners transporting attendees from the train station downtown to the peace grove for ten cents a trip. Trinket hawkers set up impromptu shops along River Road, and, at one point, a liquor stand opened in a cornfield near the meeting site to serve peace doves parched by the August heat. Merchants appealed to shoppers by advertising that the peace conference warranted purchasing a new outfit.

The *Times* reporter wrote about the 1883 scene:

> *A young man named Town or Towner delivered himself of an assorted lot of Indian stories, in which the hero was always Town or Towner. The young man was with Custer, so he said, and Custer's reputation has now been demolished wholly. Young Town or Towner now stars with the Winnemucca troupe (a reference to the Indian princess). He dispenses Winnemucca's photographs and Winnemucca's autographs at 10 cents apiece. When the young Indian historian had quieted down, Miss Nellie Bentley, the prettiest girl in all Groton, sang a little ballad, which so pleased the assemblage that they insisted on another, and another.*

For forty years following the Civil War, annual Mystic peace meetings drew thousands to the village each August. *Courtesy Mystic River Historical Society Inc., Mystic, Connecticut.*

Newspaper reports through the years noted that many of the speakers held the attention of even the largest of crowds. Other years, however, newspaper reports indicated that conference-goers were more interested in a good time than in taking their cause too seriously.

By the time of the Spanish-American War, the conferences had lost their appeal. Antigovernment protest and speeches critical of those heading into battle were not popular. In addition, locals were fed up by the drunkenness and brawling that sometimes, paradoxically, broke out on the conference grounds.

Crowds dwindled. In 1898, only a dozen wagons were reported at the conference, and by 1911, the *Hartford Courant* reported just forty-five peace conference attendees. The Universal Peace Union began looking for a buyer for the Mystic property. Mary Jobe purchased the land and operated her summer camp for girls there until the Great Depression.

Thanks to her, the site of the long-ago peace conferences was later preserved and made accessible to the public. In a way, one wish of the peace doves was granted through preservation of the site as open space and a wildlife sanctuary. It remains a place of serenity and peaceful contemplation of the type the peace conferences advocated.

SOME FIRESIDE MUSIC

Charles Phelps Williams was a member of one of Stonington's most prominent and wealthy families, one that made a fortune investing in Stonington's sealing and whaling businesses in the nineteenth century. Williams's father also established the Ocean Bank in Stonington Borough.

While the Williams name remains well known locally, one small piece of the Williams family history is less known. The twentieth-century fate of a former Williams family mansion on Montauk Avenue made for one tragicomic day in the town's history.

Charles Phelps Williams, born in 1866, lived large. He was the son and namesake of a man who was one of the most prominent shipowners and businessmen in town. The younger Williams was president of the First National Bank of Stonington while he lived in town. He also was readily recognized around town. Described as large, florid and imposing, he frequently drove his fast and well-bred horses along the town's streets. When the popularity of automobiles began to increase after the turn of the twentieth century, Williams was the first Stonington resident to own one. He also was reported to own the first speedboat in town, an Arrow, that became a local spectacle as it cruised in Stonington Harbor.

In the late 1800s, Williams built a prominent mansion on Montauk Avenue near the Stonington-Mystic Road, now Route 1. When he moved to Newport, Rhode Island, where he gained a reputation as a horse breeder and prominent horse-show judge, he sold the mansion. His former home then was converted to use as Stoneridge Country Club. By the Prohibition era, the building became a well-known speakeasy.

It was at the country club on an August day in 1933, just months before the end of Prohibition, that a fire broke out. It later was reported as one of the worst in the town's history to that date, notwithstanding several spectacular fires that had previously burned parts of downtown Mystic. Most notable about the Stoneridge fire, however, was the manner in which the fifteen club guests and twenty employees reacted to the blaze, as relayed in a local newspaper article.

Just after 6:00 p.m., someone noticed fire on the building's roof. The blaze was believed to have started in an overheated chimney. Guests quickly were warned to leave the building and remain outdoors. They didn't take these warnings seriously, however. They instead entered and left the building repeatedly to retrieve clothing and other belongings. Employees also walked in and out, carrying rolled-up rugs, expensive furnishings and objets d'art.

Local firefighters worked around the guests and employees as best they could. They laid hoses for more than a mile to pump water from the nearest body of water onto the building.

The spectacle drew more and more onlookers as time wore on. The crowd reached an estimated five thousand people, who gathered on the road and lawn to watch the firefighters work. The burgeoning audience even was treated to musical entertainment. On one of their trips into the burning building, employees retrieved the club's grand piano, rolling it onto the lawn. Musicians then played a continual medley of tunes as the grand building was reduced to ashes and rubble.

While descriptions of the scene seem akin to a farce, the fire also was a tragedy. Beyond the loss of the building, the fire killed a volunteer first responder. Despite the rather blasé reaction to the fire among club guests, forty-nine-year-old Amos Nugent understood the danger the burning building posed to spectators. Not only could the smoke and flames be deadly, but the fire could also undermine the building's stability, putting it in danger of collapse. While Nugent strove to keep people away from the six weakened forty-foot chimneys, he fell victim to a crumbling column of brick himself.

When the *Hartford Courant* reported Nugent's death on August 18, it said Nugent, who was town fire police officer, had volunteered to help with the fire lines. He succumbed to his injuries—a fractured skull and chest injuries—at Westerly Hospital in nearby Rhode Island.

Besides the human toll, the fire caused a heavy financial loss, although reports of this vary greatly. One local newspaper put the building's loss at $75,000, while another estimated it at $100,000. The *Hartford Courant* called it a $200,000 loss. Regardless, the building was not insured and wasn't rebuilt.

ADAPTING DURING PROHIBITION

On a cold winter's day in 1931, the town's commercial fishermen, who were struggling in the depths of the Great Depression, got an unanticipated financial boost from a different kind of catch in Stonington Harbor.

"A secret cache that would have made the pirates of old envious has been discovered in Davy Jones's locker—and as a result Stonington fishermen have been indulging in a new and profitable adventure, that of fishing for liquor," the *Hartford Courant* reported on February 27, 1931, under the headline "Stonington Nets Get Sunken Bottled Trove, Coast Guard Ruins Utopia."

The Stonington boats pulled dragnets full of some two hundred sacks of liquor from the waters off the village. Each sack held about two dozen pints of rye whiskey. The liquor fetched one dollar a quart at the wharf or between two and six dollars a quart if the fishermen delivered it to customers' homes. At a time when the average weekly U.S. salary stood at about twenty-six dollars, the sunken liquor sacks made for a lucrative, if short-lived, business for the fishermen.

"For a while liquor was plentiful and business depression for the fishermen was over," the *Courant* reported. "Scores of rowboats tossed on the water between the breakwater in Stonington Harbor and the west end of Wamphussic [*sic*] Point—and then along came trouble. A picket boat from the Watch Hill [Rhode Island] Coast Guard station bore down on the craft and instantly many sacks of liquor went back into the briny deep."

In 1919, the thirty-sixth state ratified a constitutional amendment banning the sale, importation, production and transportation of alcoholic beverages. Between 1920 and 1933, Prohibition was the law of the land. Both Connecticut and Rhode Island rejected the Eighteenth Amendment that led to Prohibition, but the Volstead Act still became the official law in the United States.

Theoretically, the Eighteenth Amendment transformed the United States into a dry nation. The reality, however, was that the ban simply pushed the liquor business underground and often into the hands of gangsters. For shoreline New England, Prohibition touched off frequent battles between rumrunners striving to supply a thirsty populace and the Coast Guard charged with enforcing the law.

Ship owners soon discovered that they could bring overseas liquor to a so-called Rum Row in the waters three miles offshore, just outside of the legal jurisdiction of the United States. From numerous ports, including Stonington and Mystic, smaller boats then shuttled between Rum Row and local docks, speeding through coastal waters in an effort to escape detection by the Coast Guard.

While the Coast Guard would much later come to be beloved by locals in southeastern Connecticut, during Prohibition many residents tired of the liquor ban. Beaten down financially by the Great Depression, they instead sympathized with the rumrunners. Regardless of where their sympathies lay, however, shoreline residents grew used to the impacts of bootlegging locally. It wasn't unheard of for shoreline residents, for example, to hear and see rumrunners' and Coast Guardsmen's gunshots piercing the dark waters offshore. Local boat owners turned to rum-running to make a living, and numerous local residents were arrested for bootlegging. Illegal speakeasies operated locally, including one in the basement of the William Pendleton House on Main Street in Stonington. Some local businesses such as Mystic's Lathrop Engine secured business repairing rum-running boat engines.

Although bootlegging was a dangerous pursuit, it also was lucrative enough that numerous boat owners were willing to risk it. Stonington fisherman, author and artist Ellery Thompson wrote in his book *Draggerman's Haul* about two Stonington boats—*Bird* and *Thelma Phoebe*—involved in rum-running around 1922, for example.

Throughout the 1920s and early 1930s, local newspapers reported on gun battles between rumrunners and federal agents, both on land and at sea. The *Hartford Courant* on September 22, 1922, noted that an attempted raid on rumrunners in Stonington ended with shots fired. "Rum running from motor boats, which has been going on all summer along the Stonington shore, developed an episode last night when Patrolman Thomas Connell, who detected a landing party, was blackjacked and Charles Ryan, who went to his assistance, was shot at," the *Courant* article reported.

Such violence was not isolated. The Coast Guard seized locally owned boats, and federal agents made numerous bootlegging arrests. Also in 1922, a Stonington man was fined and jailed for thirty days for bootlegging. In 1924, a raid at Lord's Point in Stonington netted more than nine hundred quarts of liquor and resulted in the arrests of two men, one local and one from Hartford.

On July 27, 1927, the *Courant* reported that a major bootlegging ring that extended throughout eastern Connecticut, including Mystic and Stonington, was being investigated. On December 8, 1928, the *Courant* reported that the Stonington boat *Porpoise* with a load of liquor was seized by New York Coast Guard officers. Five Stonington residents aboard the boat were arrested.

So, when Stonington fishermen began dragnetting loads of liquor from the bottom of the harbor in 1931, it was just another in a long list of unusual Prohibition incidents in which the potential payoff from the sale of illegal hooch was worth the risk of fine and imprisonment. Some Stonington residents ultimately paid a price in the incident. John Henry and his son Joseph were arrested and fined fifty-five dollars for petty smuggling. The liquor business also was temporarily halted as the Coast Guard patrols remained in the area.

But the fishermen were used to waiting patiently. They told the *Courant* reporter that the longer the Coast Guard thwarted further dragnetting of the bottles, the more the demand would build and the more the price per quart would rise.

"Fishermen tonight merely grinned when asked how they first learned of the submerged rye but admitted that this was by no means the first 'haul' they had made under such auspices," the *Courant* reported. "They also made it known that there were some 'babies out on Rum Row that will burn up when they hear of this'."

Police also did not easily give up. On February 28, the *Courant* reported that police were raiding Stonington homes, searching for liquor hauled from the water. "A raid was made at the home of Manuel Rodrick, a fisherman, but no liquor was found. Other raids were scheduled for the afternoon," the *Courant* reported. Still, there is little evidence of distress among local residents, Instead, the troopers' "presence added to the excitement which has prevailed, particularly in the borough, for several days."

FOR SALE: TWO GENTLY USED POLICE CARS

The town's two police cars sat idle on the front lawn of Town Hall with "for sale" signs on their windshields in the fall of 1940. Business owners begged a powerful taxpayer association to reconsider the town meeting vote that slashed the budget needed to operate the cars. But Leslie Haley of Old Mystic, president of the Taxpayers' League, responded unequivocally: "The police cars were ordered out of commission by a majority vote of the taxpayers at the annual financial town meeting. It is out of our hands to continue any further discussion about them."

For many years throughout the twentieth century, Stonington's annual budget battles became a given. They pitted residents striving to keep property taxes in check against advocates for public services such as education, public safety, social services and library services. It was not unusual for budgets to require three or more townwide referendum votes to be approved. But the budget battle of 1940 may have been one of the most dramatic in the town's history, with a powerful government watchdog group digging in its heels, the sidelined police cars making for eye-catching photographs in local newspapers and a seriously injured accident victim pleading from his hospital bed that police cars be returned to patrol.

At the heart of the battle was a group called the Taxpayers League. According to one undated account in *The Day* of New London, the league advocated budget cuts in 1939 that had crippled the town's operations. A special town meeting was conducted later that year to appropriate enough money to prevent a local government shutdown.

In 1940, the league again lobbied for drastic cuts. At the October town meeting lasting four and a half hours and attended by some seven hundred residents, the league and its supporters garnered enough votes to slash $6,750 from the budget, nearly 2 percent of the total spending plan. "The salary of the first selectman was slashed, a vote was passed to put the town police cars up for sale and the unemployment and almshouse appropriations were cut," *The Day* reported. Only the education budget was spared.

Soon after the vote, officials parked the town's two police cars in a prominent location in front of Town Hall and displayed "for sale" signs on their windshields.

Local business owners were not happy. They called the cuts draconian and began working to reverse them. Within a few days of the town meeting vote, business owners from the town's three main villages of Pawcatuck, Mystic and Stonington Borough pleaded with Taxpayers

League members to bring the budget back for another vote. Among the business owners were Otto Seidner, whose mayonnaise was made and bottled in Westerly, and Leo H. Higgins, a highly respected member of the Pawcatuck business community and owner of the longtime landmark Higgins pharmacy.

A planned meeting among business owners and members of the league was announced. A day later, however, Haley said no such meeting would be conducted. The league's executive committee was firmly opposed to reopening the police car funding issue. "We wish to tell you that this action at the town meeting was well considered from every angle, and a comprehensive poll taken of voters from each district before said resolution was presented," Haley wrote to the business owners. "Therefore, we feel any further debate on the subject by us would be more than futile."

Shortly after Haley sent the letter, John LaFountain, a resident who was hospitalized in Westerly, Rhode Island, following a serious automobile accident, talked to reporters from his hospital bed. Had the cars been sidelined at the time of his accident, LaFountain said, he might not have survived. Only because the police responded so quickly to the Stonington Road accident was he able to get necessary medical attention in a timely fashion. LaFountain noted that he was "against wasting the town's funds in any way but in the case of the police cars, I believe it to be money well spent."

LaFountain's doctor also spoke up. He, too, was convinced that the police cars were necessary to protect residents.

Enough Stonington residents agreed with LaFountain. A special town meeting to reconsider the funding was scheduled for mid-November.

The Taxpayers League was not ready to give up, however. It issued a statement accusing its opponents of underhanded tactics. Haley said that while opponents accused the league of controlling the town meeting "like a burlesque," "the meetings that were held prior to the formation of this league might better be called tragedies."

Haley and his group also used only thinly veiled bigoted statements in an attempt to garner more support. He noted that the league was made up of "native Americans" while many of the business owners were from the town's immigrant communities. Haley also called his opponents "political bloodsuckers," insinuating that they were taking kickbacks to oppose the league.

"While there are possibly one or two on this police car committee who are really sincere, it would seem that the most of them are associated with the same clique who continually agitated until the mammoth monument to

Left: Railroad bridge over West Broad Street, Pawcatuck. *Courtesy Westerly Library & Wilcox Park.*

Below: Stonington High School in 1959. The school was built at its current location in the 1950s. *Courtesy collection of the Stonington Historical Society.*

a townspeople's folly was built in Pawcatuck—the new high school," Haley said, referring to the recently completed school.

Just two days after the league's nasty statement was published in the local press, *The Day* newspaper reported a new rumor: the league would commandeer the special town meeting to make even further cuts, this time seeking to reduce police personnel.

On November 12, a crowd attended the special town meeting. By a vote of 416 to 136, residents restored police car funding and even expanded the fleet by one car. This allowed for patrols dedicated to each of the town's three major villages. "Taxpayers League Is Given Crushing Defeat at Special Meeting," a headline in a local paper proclaimed.

One contentious budget fight was over. Many more budget battles were still to come.

A Factional Feud

Stonington has been described as a collection of distinct and independent villages loosely tied together as a municipal entity. Pawcatuck, Stonington Borough—incorporated in 1801 and now the state's oldest borough—and Mystic all maintain individual identities and uber-local community loyalty.

This divided loyalty has led to countless clashes over a variety of municipal issues. During the Great Depression, these village rivalries came to a head in an extended public dispute over where to locate the town's high school and athletic fields.

During the 1930s, Stonington High School was located in the stately Borough School building constructed in 1888. The Second Empire–style brick building with its distinctive four-story entrance tower housed elementary, middle school and high school students. But by the Depression era, more and more residents considered the forty-plus-year-old building outdated for use by high schoolers. They also thought that the popular high school sports teams were not adequately accommodated on the small fields not far from the school.

Discussion about the future of the high school and its athletic facilities began calmly enough. In May 1933, a local newspaper reported that Stonington's Lions Club favored a plan promoted by a local property owner. Mrs. Herbert D. Owen requested property-tax exemption for fifteen years in exchange for giving the town a piece of her land for use as high school athletic fields. The school's football and baseball teams already played and practiced there.

By the time of an April 1934 financial town meeting, residents' emotions had reached a boiling point on the issue. The *Stonington Mirror* on April 28 reported that contingents of residents from both Pawcatuck and Mystic turned out in force to oppose the purchase of Owen's field. After much debate, two separate athletic-field purchase proposals were tabled indefinitely. One parcel was Owen's field. The other parcel was near Wequetequock, closer to Pawcatuck. "The stormiest town meeting in many years was closed to stroke of the gavel at 11 o'clock, and as the citizens left the hall small groups gathering in front of the building to continue their personal arguments over the matter of the athletic fields, two of them coming to blows over the matter," the *Mirror* article reported.

Just two months later, another possible athletic field site in Pawcatuck added to the controversy. A two-hundred-acre parcel off what is now known as Route 1 was also on the table. This land is the current site of Stonington

High School and its athletic fields. The town boards of selectmen, finance and education agreed to purchase this tract, called the Mandell property. "After the legal requirements have been taken care of, a town meeting will be called to vote on the proposition," a local newspaper reported on June 29. "Judging from the talk of our citizens this latter will be a mere formality, and in the near future the town will take possession."

It would not prove so easy to resolve the issue, however.

Yet another parcel of land adjacent to the Mandell property also became available, and town leaders sought to buy it as a possible future high school site. Borough loyalists would not hear of this. In August 1934, they led a contingent of borough residents to defeat the proposal in a 72–54 town meeting vote. In September, a temporary fix for high school athletes was announced: Mrs. Owen said that she agreed to again rent her field for use by the high school football team.

Buying the Mandell property and land nearby it was not a dead issue, however. In April 1935, residents of Mystic and Pawcatuck forged an alliance supporting purchase of the Mandell property for $4,000. Borough residents countered with a petition for the town to buy Owen Field for $5,000.

The Mandell land supporters issued a statement contending that Stonington High School athletes had for too long been hindered by the lack of adequate fields. "Good judges are of the opinion that, with an expenditure of $2,000 in improvements one of the best sports fields in the State can be equipped," the statement read in part. "The land lies ideally for baseball and football fields, a running track and tennis courts. There are also beautiful wooded sites for scout camps and picnic grounds." In addition, the Depression had decreased land values, making the purchase a bargain.

On April 15, more than 1,000 residents gathered at what the *Westerly Sun* labeled a "stormy session." A headline on its article read, "Campaign Bitterly Waged between Pawcatuck and Borough Sections." The meeting was preceded by some street theater. An estimated 175 borough men and boys, joined by the fire department's drum and fife corps, paraded through borough streets and into Town Hall. Marchers beat on tin cans, and police officers called to the scene asked about 50 young boys, and later another 50 high schoolers, to vacate Town Hall seats to allow more room for other residents.

"Over 1,000 rabidly partisan voters jammed in the Town Hall to take part in the battle between the supporters of the Stonington Road [Pawcatuck] proposition and the Boroughites who were intent on purchasing Owen Field," the article reported. "The 600 seats were filled long before 8 o'clock, the time for the start of the meeting, and standing room was at a premium.

Nearly 200 were unable to get into the hall at all. The meeting resolved itself into a test of strength between Pawcatuck and the Borough."

After more theatrics over the choice of meeting moderator, a proposal to buy the Stonington Road property for $4,000 and spend another $2,000 on improvements was put on the floor. "And then the demonstration began," the *Sun* article reported. "The borough contingent in the front rows shouted and howled at the mere suggestion of buying the former Mandell property." The article continues: "Moderator Palmer, who started his duties in a business-like manner and seemed for a few minutes to be able to handle the situation, was soon engulfed in uncertainty by the bickering and heckling of his own supporters from the borough and general confusion reigned."

The Pawcatuck contingent finally won in a 473-to-380 vote. Almost as soon as the athletic-field matter was put to rest, however, factions again began forming over a possible new high school. At yet another heavily attended town meeting in October 1935, residents accepted a federal grant to build a school on the same site as the athletic fields. By the end of the month, a town meeting attended by 1,200 people rescinded the earlier vote.

Almost immediately, Pawcatuck residents began circulating petitions to restore the original vote. As the 1936 school year began with even more students jammed into classrooms, the state's supervisor of secondary education assessed the cost to build as many as three new schools in town as a possible solution to the factional fighting. Nearly half the town's students then lived in Pawcatuck, and the other half were split between Mystic and Stonington.

In November 1936, residents again were at a town meeting. "Town Meeting Lively as Old Question Comes up to Harass Weary Voters at Long Session," the headline in the November 25 edition of the *Stonington Mirror* read. "During the meeting several attempts were made to either block or change the original proposal, on grounds that a central high school should be built nearer the center of town than in Pawcatuck." That meeting again approved a plan for a new high school in Pawcatuck, although the site in question was now in the heart of downtown Pawcatuck. Only Pawcatuck students would attend classes there.

Borough residents were not ready to give up. In February, the issue was again headed to a town meeting vote, even as Pawcatuck leaders threatened to secede from the town if the plan was not put to rest. Interestingly enough, by this time, more residents of the borough and Mystic favored building the high school at the former Mandell property. Pawcatuck again prevailed at the town meeting. By September, plans for a two-story, nineteen-classroom

Train wreck near Stonington Borough after the September 1938 hurricane. *Courtesy collection of the Stonington Historical Society.*

high school located on the former Moss farm at the crest of a hill overlooking downtown Pawcatuck and Westerly, Rhode Island, were progressing.

Ironically, it was the federal government that solved the local quandary of where Stonington's high school students would attend classes—at least temporarily. The government announced late that fall that it would grant money for the Pawcatuck school only if the Borough School also was demolished. Federal officials considered the Borough School's top floor unsafe. After some negotiation, federal and local officials compromised. All of the town's high schoolers would attend classes at the new Pawcatuck school, and only the Borough School's top floor would be closed. Younger students would continue lessons on the lower levels.

By June 1938, construction began in Pawcatuck. The building was expected to open by February 1939. Then, the tremendous New England hurricane struck in September 1938, damaging the unfinished structure and again delaying the school's opening.

Finally, on September 1, 1939, a local newspaper reported that the new Stonington High School would open on September 6. The six-year struggle finally appeared settled. Pawcatuck won this scrappy battle among the villages. The victory would be short lived, however. A little more than a decade later, a new Stonington High School was built at its current location.

A Great Storm

On the unseasonably warm and humid afternoon of September 21, 1938, some six hundred children at one of the town's largest schools were gathering books and papers in anticipation of dismissal. The fifty-eight ninth-graders at West Broad Street School in the village of Pawcatuck were dismissed at their regular time of 2:15 p.m., but by the time the younger children prepared to leave about an hour later, the wind that teachers had noticed increasing throughout the afternoon was howling with unprecedented fury. Rain was pelting the building.

At 3:30 p.m., Principal Katharine B. Crandall instructed the school's eighteen teachers to keep children in their classrooms until the storm abated. "We waited 10 minutes and then the storm broke in all its fury," Crandall later wrote in part of her end-of-school-year report to the town's board of education. "We now realized that this was not a normal storm."

Indeed, the Great New England Hurricane of 1938 was no normal gale. Forecasters aware of the mammoth storm plowing north through the Atlantic Ocean in the previous days did not adequately warn New Englanders about its potential danger. The notion that a tropical storm would hit New England seemed preposterous at the time. So, when it did hit, local residents were not prepared.

The storm had winds of well over one hundred miles per hour and caused a tremendous storm surge that brought catastrophic flooding throughout New England. Some seven hundred people died. Whole beach communities were wiped off the map. The shoreline was permanently altered. Millions of dollars' worth of damage occurred. Fires touched off by the storm left large swaths of New London in ruins. Parts of Rhode Island beach cottages, and the people clinging to them, ended up on Stonington shores. Flooding in the borough stranded train traffic and made for some heroic rescues on the part of train porters. The storm's unbridled force and powerful winds, combined with surging water, scooped up what today is known as Sandy Point, moving it across Little Narragansett Bay from Watch Hill, Rhode Island, to its new home in Stonington. It was perhaps the most striking example of the storm's power to reshape the landscape. Today, Sandy Point is overseen by the Stonington Community Center and is a popular summer destination for local boaters.

While these more dramatic stories played out during the storm, the events at West Broad Street School show that the storm impacted everyone in town. Many of West Broad's students walked to and from school because they lived nearby, within the densely populated downtown village area. Katharine Crandall realized the folly of sending children as young as five out amid the crashing tree limbs and collapsing power lines. She ordered the children out of the hallways and back into their classrooms. And when the furious winds began threatening to smash the school's towering windows that were designed to allow a maximum of natural light into each classroom, teachers began leading the children down to the school's lowest level, a semi-basement area.

Before all the children could be brought safely down the stairs, the hurricane blew out a first-floor window. A fourth-grader, Marjorie Miner, was hit by a flying shard of glass. Her leg was cut severely.

Crandall asked a seventh-grade teacher, Catherine Cogan, to try to get the girl to Dr. Samuel S. Farago's office at 101 West Broad Street. Cogan was chosen because she was among the few teachers who had an automobile. It was parked on nearby Moss Street.

Two eighth-grade boys, Edmund Adams and Calvert Lewis, were recruited to carry the injured girl to the car, and Cogan set off to find the doctor. Katharine Crandall later wrote in her report that the teacher did not find the doctor in his office and so took the girl to the hospital in Westerly, Rhode Island, about two miles away. The teacher remained with

A boat wrecked on Gravel Street in Mystic after the September 1938 hurricane. *Courtesy Mystic River Historical Society Inc., Mystic, Connecticut.*

Top: Wreckage on West Mystic Avenue in Mystic after the September 1938 hurricane. *Courtesy Mystic River Historical Society Inc., Mystic, Connecticut.*

Bottom: West Broad Street School in Pawcatuck served as a public school for nearly 120 years. *Photo taken by author.*

the injured girl until about 10:00 p.m. Miner ended up being hospitalized for about two weeks.

At the school, teachers and students tried to make the best of the tense situation. As wires fell, telephones and electricity were knocked out. Teachers led the students in a sing-along to try to buoy spirits and quell fears. Among the tunes were "Pack Up Your Troubles in Your Old Kit Bag."

Occasionally, parents braving the storm appeared at the school to claim their children. When the storm subsided by early evening, many children were dismissed to return to their homes, but then the school became a shelter for whole families whose streets and houses were flooded.

The owner of a nearby boardinghouse, a Mr. Loudon, came to the school at about 8:30 p.m. to offer refuge. Crandall and the remaining families left the school and headed across West Broad Street to the boardinghouse for the night.

After the storm, Crandall and the other school administrators in town were asked to assess the damage to their buildings. At West Broad, "Fourteen windows blew in, three classroom skylights were broken, the skylight in the assembly hall was broken and bricks fell from the dormers on the third floor." The hurricane made for some tense hours for the large group of children and teachers huddled in the school's unlit basement, but the principal's decision to keep the pupils at school likely saved children's lives.

AFTERWORD

While the children at West Broad Street School may have initially recalled the 1938 hurricane as a tense but exciting adventure, that feeling would give way to the realization that the storm had extracted a terrible toll. Hundreds of lives were lost, and the storm's deadly force forever changed the region.

At different times in the ever-evolving history of Stonington and Mystic, those who lived here were forced to confront their share of natural disasters and other life-changing situations. Many, such as the nation's Civil War, had their origins far beyond local boundaries. Still, the impact was keenly felt here.

While most communities face significant events of their own, not all can match what happened here. Stonington and Mystic can point to some level of involvement in just about every significant national event or movement that would transform our country in its formative years. The British bombarded these shorefront communities in both the Revolutionary War and the War of 1812, what some historians call the Second Revolutionary War.

In the early years here, slavery was practiced, as was the organized resistance known as the abolitionist movement. The industrial revolution spread here from its North American start in nearby Rhode Island. Mass immigration from a variety of European countries was likewise a defining experience locally.

It could be argued that the brutal treatment of indigenous peoples that came to characterize the young nation's relationship with the people who

The first trolley arrives in the village of Old Mystic. *Courtesy Indian & Colonial Research Center Incorporated, Old Mystic, Connecticut.*

Mills lined both sides of the Pawcatuck River in the early 1900s. *Courtesy Westerly Library & Wilcox Park.*

Workers line up outside Pawcatuck's Victor Company. *Courtesy Westerly Library & Wilcox Park.*

lived here before the Europeans "discovered" America had its origins in the Pequot War (1637–38). That war, of course, began in Mystic.

In all of these events, and others, the people of Stonington and Mystic adapted to meet the challenges of changing times. Each significant change and pivotal event created a new normal and provided the building blocks for the future in these communities that seem to be forever on the move.

Transformation keeps communities vital, and Stonington and Mystic are among Connecticut's most vital. Whether it's through dedicated village loyalty or in other forms of civic involvement, the people who call these places home today honor the legacy of previous generations when they actively engage in community life. Whether they are reacting to contemporary challenges or simply living their lives according to their own desires, they are helping shape a present that will, in turn, help future generations shape their times. Those stories, big or seemingly small, need to be told, and that is what I set out to do.

BIBLIOGRAPHY

Books

Brown, Barbara W., and James M. Rose. *Tapestry: A Living History of the Black Family in Southeastern Connecticut*. New London, CT: New London County Historical Society, 1979.

Calabretta, Fred, ed. *Fishing Out of Stonington*. Mystic, CT: Mystic Seaport, 1970.

Clarke, Helen May. *An Account of My Life: The Childhood Journals of Helen May Clarke of Mystic, Connecticut*. Mystic, CT: Mystic River Historical Society, 1997.

Cuffe, Paul. *Narrative of the Life and Adventures of Paul Cuffe, a Pequot Indian*. Horace N. Bill, 1839.

Cutler, Carl C. *Mystic: The Story of a Small New England Seaport*. Mystic, CT: Mystic Seaport Museum, 1980.

Druett, Joan, ed. *She Was a Sister Sailor, Mary Brewster's Whaling Journals, 1845–1851*. Mystic, CT: Mystic Seaport Museum, 1992.

The First Hundred Years: Pawcatuck Seventh Day Baptist Church, 1840–1940. Westerly, RI: Utter Company, 1940.

Haynes, Williams. *Captain George and Lady Ann, the Denisons of Pequotsepos Manor*. Mystic, CT: Denison Society, undated.

———. *Stonington Chronology 1649–1949*. Guilford, CT: Pequot Press, 1949.

Inderfurth, Karl H. *Back When*. Mystic, CT: Mystic Publications, 1995.

Kimball, Carol. *Historic Glimpses, Recollections of Days Past in the Mystic River Valley*. Mystic, CT: Flat Hammock Press, 2005.

MacDonald, Gail Braccidiferro. *West Broad Street School: A Century of Education in Pawcatuck*." Pawcatuck, CT: 2000.

Palmer, Henry Robinson. *Stonington by the Sea*. Stonington, CT: Palmer Press, 1913.

Shoemaker, Nancy. *Living with Whales, Documents and Oral Histories of Native New England Whaling History*. Amherst: University of Massachusetts Press, 2014.

———. *Native American Whalemen and the World*. Chapel Hill: University of North Carolina Press, 2015.

Strother, Horatio T. *The Underground Railroad in Connecticut*. Middletown, CT: Wesleyan University Press, 1962.

Thompson, Ellery. *Draggerman's Haul*. Westerly, RI: Book & Tackle Shop, 1994.

Interviews

Comrie, Marilyn. February 2018.

Dickson, Ernie. July 31, 2001.

Erskine, David, director, Stonington Historical Society. Several dates, 2018.

Higgins, Blanche, Westerly-Pawcatuck history expert. April 23, 2018.

O'Keefe, Larry, St. Michael Church historian. March 30, 2018.

Suppicich, Robert, director, Stonington Historical Society. October 19, 2018.

Wood, Elizabeth, executive director, Stonington Historical Society. October 15, 2018.

Woods, J. Cedric, director, Institute for New England Native American Studies, University of Massachusetts. April 2018.

Letters, Papers and Miscellaneous Documents

Akeley, Mary Jobe. Letters and papers, Linda Lear Center for Special Collections and Archives, Connecticut College.

"Captain Paul Cuffe: His Work, Vision, and Living Legacy." Exhibit. New Bedford Whaling Museum, New Bedford, Massachusetts.

Coelho, Walter. "The Economic Importance of Whaling Out of Stonington Village: 1821–1892." July 6, 1975.

————. "Stonington Whaling Fleet." Thesis, Central Connecticut State College, February 17, 1971.

Cohn, Joan. "Old Mystic Schools in Bygone Days." Indian & Colonial Research Center, Old Mystic, Connecticut, November 15, 1997.

Mystic River Historical Society files, Mystic, Connecticut.
> Akeley, Mary Jobe
> Camp Mystic
> Eldredge, Charles Q.
> Mystic Oral School
> Mystic Peace Meetings
> Rossie Velvet Mill

Oral Histories Stonington Fishing Fleet, Mystic Seaport, Connecticut.
> Berg, Doris
> Pater, Ann Maderia
> Rita, Ann M.
> Volovar, Vivian

Richardson, Mary. "The American Velvet Co., the Rossie Velvet Co., 1890–1940." April 26, 1990.

Stonington Historical Society Files
> African Americans
> American Velvet
> Brewster, Mary
> Gabriel, Claude and Jenkins, Prudence
> German Club
> *Historical Footnotes* newsletter articles, various dates and topics
> Railroad
> Squadrito, Anthony
> Stonington Community Center
> Stonington Poor Farm
> Third Baptist Church
> Wadawanuck Hotel

"Stonington Industries, 1649–1949." Tricentennial committee booklet. Stonington Tercentenary Committee, 1949.

Walling's Route and City Guides—Stonington Line, New York to Boston. Taintor Brother Press, n.d.

Westerly, Rhode Island Library. Local History Room files.
> Whistler, George Washington

"Whalers Out of Mystic." Marine Historical Association, Mystic, Connecticut, n.d.

Whistler Collection. The Hunterian. University of Glasgow, Scotland.

Yale Indian Papers Project.

Committee reports relative to Groton Indians, May 23, 1766; October 11, 1766.

Complaint of Pequot Indians against Groton, no date, eighteenth century; May 1722.

Newspaper, Newsletter and Magazine Articles

Catlin, Roger. "4 Corners: A Look at Life on the Edges of Connecticut Finds Diversity." *Hartford Courant*, August 30, 1987.

Columbian Register (New Haven, CT). "Negro Suffrage Election." October 7, 1865.

Comrie, Marilyn. "Orchard House: Inn Catered to Blacks in the Era of Segregation." *Westerly Sun*, February 20, 1994.

Cox, Diane, "Collector's Legacy: A Living Past." *New York Times*, November 20, 1983.

Davis, Neil A., "A Slave Named Venture." *Hartford Courant*, December 10, 1972.

The Day (New London, CT). "Auction Off the Lower Pawcatuck Village." May 13, 1937.

———. "Mystic—300 Years." July 7, 1954.

———. "Only Watchmen Remain at Closed Thread Mill." April 19, 1939.

———. "Stiles H.F. Ross Oldest Resident Dies at 96." July 6, 1954.

Dufresne, Bethe. "A Little Museum Gets Noticed." *The Day*, February 13, 2000.

Evening Star (Dunedin, NZ). "James Apes, Whaler and Shearer." October 9, 1938.

Griffith, Owen. "Do-It-Yourself Golf Course." *Hartford Courant*, June 7, 1959.

Hartford Courant. "Arguments Heard on Contested Will of C.P. Williams." May 5, 1938.

———. "Body of Heroic Porter Found Near Stonington." October 20, 1938.

———. "Bootlegger Jailed as Drunken Driver Has Customer List." January 20, 1926.

———. "Building Boom Strikes Mystic." December 30, 1905.

———. "Captured Rum Launch Is Stonington Craft." December 8, 1928.

———. "Caught in Shafting." July 12, 1901.

————. "Chinaman Came to Stonington in 1859." December 23, 1912.

————. "Close Velvet Plant Because of Strike." June 10, 1917.

————. "Coast Guard Bullets Halt Speed Boats." October 25, 1930.

————. "Estate Left by Daniel Denison." January 26, 1912.

————. "Fisherman Ordered to Leave U.S." March 10, 1954.

————. "Hartford Man Held for Rum Running." August 17, 1924.

————. "Here's a Town That Has Two Sabbaths." November 2, 1913.

————. "Higganum Man Writes of Slaves' Escape Road." May 6, 1962.

————. "More Arrests in Rum Ring Are Pending." July 24, 1927.

————. "Mrs. S.B. Butler Dies; Indian Scholar." June 21, 1969.

————. "Mystic Oral School: State Board of Charities Condemns It." April 2, 1897.

————. "Mystic's One-Man Museum." December 19, 1926.

————. "Opposed to Force." August 22, 1895.

————. "Peace Lovers Meet at Mystic Peace Grove." August 18, 1911.

————. "Petition of Slaves in Connecticut for Their Freedom." July 5, 1847.

————. "Police Search Homes in Stonington for Best Rum Row Rye." February 28, 1931.

————. "Rum Runners Assaulted Officer." September 12, 1922.

————. "6 Poisoned by Whiskey." April 11, 1910.

————. "Stonington Man Fined $200 as Bootlegger." October 26, 1922.

————. "Stonington Native 'Last of the Mohicans.'" November 20, 1927.

————. "Stonington Negro Church Sold at Public Auction," May 16, 1926.

————. "Stonington Nets Get Sunken Bottled Trove, Coast Guard Ruins Utopia." February 27, 1931.

————. "Stonington Policeman, Injured in Fire, Dies." August 18, 1933.

————. "A Thousand Eels." January 10, 1918.

————. "The Wadawanuck House—A Quiet and Pleasant Resort." August 9, 1875.

Hileman, Maria. "Mystic Shipyard Tied to Freedom Trail." *The Day*, December 26, 2000.

Hinshaw, John V. "Third Stonington: The Afro-American Church on Water Street." *Historical Footnotes*. Stonington Historical Society, May 1992.

Kimball, Carol. "The Peace Meeting Doves," Historical Footnotes, Stonington Historical Society, May 1971.

————. "Peace Sanctuary Was Born in Wake of Civil War Carnage," *The Day*, May 17, 2001.

Kravsow, Irving. "An Inspiring Career in Faith." *Hartford Courant*, April 14, 1957.

Lewis, Donald. "Stonington's Portuguese Fishermen." *Historical Footnotes,* August 1965. Stonington Historical Society.

Madeira, Mary. "Captain St. Peter, from 'Des Islas' to Stonington: The Story of Manuel Madeira and His Wife Connie." *Historical Footnotes,* August 1973. Stonington Historical Society.

Mancini, Jason. "New London's Indian Mariners." *Connecticut Explored* (Spring 2009).

Mancini, Juli. "Charles Q. Eldredge: The Historical Peacock." *Patch,* March 11, 2011.

New York Times. "Mary J. Akeley, an Explorer." July 22, 1966.

———. "Mrs. Akeley's African Journey." December 6, 1936.

———. "The Mystic Peace Meeting." August 23, 1883.

———. "Universal Peace Jubilee." August 24, 1898.

———. "Universal Peace Union." August 25, 1898.

———. "Universal Peace Union at Mystic." July 18, 1897.

———. "Universal Peace Wanted." August 25, 1883.

———. "War in a Peace Loving Town." October 27, 1884.

Otago Daily Times (New Zealand). "Mr. Himi Hipi (obituary)." August 1, 1938.

Peet, Martha Dennison. "My Home in Connecticut 50 Years Ago." *Bulletin of the Connecticut Historical Society,* January 1946.

Smith, Donald W. "Connecticut Past Lives in Old Mystic." *Hartford Courant,* October 3, 1948.

———. "Floundering in the Fog." *Hartford Courant,* July 11, 1937.

Sommer, Carol. "An Old Mystic Original." *The Day,* May 6, 2018.

Thomas, H.F. "The Story of the Stonington Railroad." *Connecticut Circle,* December 1944.

Williams, Marshall. "Abolitionist George Greenman Lived His Faith: His Home Was a Stop on Underground Railroad." *Mystic River Press,* February 15, 2007.

Information about police car budget fight comes from numerous newspaper articles clipped from unidentifiable publications, 1940.

Information about Stonington High School and athletic fields comes from numerous newspaper articles clipped from unidentifiable publications, February 5, 1931, to February 2, 1951.

INDEX

W

About the Author

Gail Braccidiferro MacDonald is a journalism faculty member at the University of Connecticut and a veteran journalist who has won numerous awards for her work. She is a Connecticut native with a deep interest in history and how historical events shape the present and future. She is the author of *Morton F. Plant and the Connecticut Shoreline: Philanthropy in the Gilded Age*, published by The History Press. She lives in New London, Connecticut, with her husband.

Visit us at
www.historypress.com